FLY FISHING

Generations of propaganda have convinced many people that fly fishing is so complicated and difficult that years of close study and expert tuition are necessary to master it. This is quite untrue. If you have the temperament for it, and if you study this book and use your common sense, you can become a reasonably proficient fly fisher in your very first season.

The whole object of this book is to encourage novices to take up their rods with confidence and boldness. Every stage of the art is covered, from building the rod through casting the fly to grassing the fish. And the enthusiasm of the author is as delightful and instructive as his encylopaedic knowledge of the subject.

TEACH YOURSELF BOOKS

Professor A. A. Luce of Trinity College, Dublin, distinguished philosopher and fisherman of long experience writes of this book:

'A pocket encyclopaedia of all forms of fly fishing practised in the British Isles, not excluding dapping. Salmon receive considerable attention, and sea trout and grayling are not neglected. The emphasis falls, quite rightly, on wet-fly and dry-fly fishing for brown trout. Every stage is covered from the building of the rod to the grassing of the fish. The instructions for learning the difficult art of casting are admirable; so too are the author's views on *purism* in angling.'

FLY FISHING

Maurice Wiggin

TEACH YOURSELF BOOKS
Hodder and Stoughton

First printed 1958
Second edition 1972
Eighth impression 1984

By the same author

THE PASSIONATE ANGLER	LIFE WITH BADGER
FISHING FOR BEGINNERS	THE ANGLER'S BEDSIDE BOOK
MY COURT CASEBOOK	THE MEMOIRS OF A MAVERICK
IN SPITE OF THE PRICE OF HAY	A COTTAGE IDYLL
TROUBLED WATERS	SEA FISHING FOR BEGINNERS
MY LIFE ON WHEELS	FACES AT THE WINDOW

ISBN 0 340 166770

Printed in Great Britain
for Hodder and Stoughton Educational,
a division of Hodder and Stoughton Ltd.,
Mill Road, Dunton Green, Sevenoaks, Kent
by Richard Clay (The Chaucer Press), Ltd., Bungay, Suffolk

To

LEONARD RUSSELL and LEONARD CUTTS
the perspicacious and pertinacious
impresarios who between them talked me
into writing this book.

PREFACE

Man in Bookshop: Why write another book about fly fishing? Aren't there enough already?

Author: There are a great many, some of them very fine. But most of them might have been written with the specific intention of putting off the beginner. Experts tend to write for experts, and the result, too often, is intimidating to the novice.

Man in Bookshop: Well, now, I'm a novice. I know nothing about fly fishing and I don't know anyone who will show me. Do you mean to tell me that I can pick it up from a book?

Author: I'm sure you can. The whole object of this book is to encourage complete novices to embark boldly on what I believe to be most satisfying, the most elegant, the most nearly artistic mode of angling. It is written throughout on the assumption that the reader comes to the subject with ordinary intelligence and total ignorance.

Man in Bookshop: That's me, I guess. But, surely, fly fishing is so complicated and difficult that you need years of close study and expert tuition to master it?

Author: There you are! Generations of propaganda have done their work. That is precisely the myth that fly fishers like to put about. Of course, it's nice and flattering. But it's quite untrue. Fly fishing is quite easy to master—if you have the temperament for it. Some haven't. I will say this: if you study this book and use your common sense, you can become a reasonably proficient fly fisher in your very first season. True, you will go on improving every year—and your pleasure will increase with increasing experience. But you can start catching fish right away.

CONTENTS

CHAPTER 1

What Is Fly Fishing?

There are three branches of rod-and-line angling: bait fishing, spinning, and fly fishing. Bait fishing explains itself. It consists of impaling a bait on a hook and putting it in the water, in the hope, if not the expectation, that a fish will take the bait into its mouth. Spinning consists of casting out a lure which represents, or is believed to represent, a small fish. The moment you have cast it out, you begin to reel it in. The lure is equipped with fins, or vanes, or is merely bent curiously, with the result that as you draw it through the water it spins; though, to be accurate, many spinning lures do not spin at all, but wobble, or lurch. Whether true spinners, or wobblers, or lurchers, they are all designed to simulate a small, injured fish trying to escape from a pursuer. It is your hope that this sad spectacle will induce some robust and pitiless predatory fish to seize the injured party.

You will see that spinning is a good deal more active and enterprising than bait fishing. Fly fishing goes even farther. Of all forms of angling, fly fishing is the most nearly an art. It is the most elegant and (to many) the most satisfying of all methods of taking fish. I would rather fish the bait than not fish at all, and I would rather spin than fish the bait; but I would rather fish the fly than either.

'Fish the fly?' A strange phrase. It has nothing to do with bluebottles and house-flies. The 'fly' in fly fishing refers to the water-born insects on which many fishes feed. There is a great variety of insects which hatch out from the water. In each of several stages of their development these aquatic insects provide food for fish —and some fish, including, heaven be praised, trout, often seem actually to prefer the aquatic insect to other and commoner forms of food; such as their own young. These, then, are the flies of the fly fisher.

My friend John Pézare, to whom I am indebted for most of the illustrations in this book—though, to be sure, he is also indebted to me—has drawn a diagram

FIG. 1. Life Cycle of an Aquatic Fly.

which shows, very roughly, the life-cycle of the typical aquatic insect. The eggs are laid (as a rule) on the surface of the water. They drift down to the bottom, or at least they submerge. They are often sticky, and they adhere in countless numbers to the stems of weeds and other aquatic vegetation. (Some female flies swim down under water to 'stick' their eggs to weeds.) Some get right down to the bottom and adhere to gravel, stones, rocks; or merely sink into the mud.

There they remain for a long time. It may be a year, it may be two. Eventually the egg becomes the larva. Eventually the larva changes into the nymph. The nymph, though still tubular and, very roughly speaking, grub-like, has got its legs and/or antennae free of the grub-case. It can swim, after a fashion, wriggling its body and waving its legs.

It swims most desperately towards the surface, towards the light of day. Rising and falling, and ever drifting with the current, it makes its precarious way towards the surface film. With a great effort it breaks through the film and sits upon the surface as the wings burst out of the grub-case. The fly is hatched.

Recognisably a fly, an insect with a body and legs and wings, it sits on the surface film, for a short period varying between seconds and long minutes. In the air the wings spread and dry. Now it is ready to fly away.

If not taken by a fish, or a bird, the fly flies. It does not fly far. It probably flies to the nearest bush or tree or clump of grass. It clings to this, waiting for the next stage in this miraculous transformation from egg to grub, from grub to flying insect. As it dries, it sheds the dull cases which covered its wings and tails and emerges in the gossamer, diaphanous beauty of the perfect insect. When fully rested, it takes to flight.

Its career as a flying insect may be as short as a day or two, or as long as a week. Eventually it reaches the apex of its brief life. The males mate with the females, after a mating ceremony, rising and falling in the air in a beautiful ritual dance. The act of mating completed, the males disappear. They die on land. The female flies back to the water. Dipping down to the surface, she lays her precious cargo of fertilised eggs on the surface. Her purpose is achieved, her life is over. Slowly the erect and lovely wings droop until they lie flat on the surface. The eggs begin their journey to an anchorage, the whole cycle starts again.

Fish feed on these aquatic flies at several stages in their development. As the *nymph* breaking loose from its anchorage and swimming up towards the surface; as the insect hatching out and resting on the surface (when it is called a *dun*); as the female returning to lay her eggs (the *spinner*); and as the dead spinner inert on the surface—in all these stages the aquatic fly provides a morsel which some fish seem to like.

The fly fisher seeks to represent such flies, at various stages in their development. He fashions his representations of various materials, fur and feather, tinsel and silk and plastic substances and wire and hair and cellulose. He ties his *artificial fly* to a gut or nylon *cast* and ties the cast to the end of his *line* and throws it out over the water. If he is successful in deceiving a fish into believing that his artificial fly is a real, natural one, the fish takes it into his mouth, and is thereupon hooked.

That is the essence of fly fishing.

CHAPTER 2

Flies that Never Flew

It is true of fly fishing, more perhaps than of any other branch of angling, that no sooner have you made a flat statement than you have to qualify it. This is going to be my principal trouble in writing this book. But it cannot be dodged. If there is one thing surer than another, it is that dogmatism and fly fishing go ill together.

FIG. 2. Hardy's Ythan Lure.

I have just given you a child's-primer résumé of what I had the temerity to call 'the essence of fly fishing'. It was true so far as it went, and I put it first in order to explain this odd word, *fly*. But, in fact, there is another sort of fly fishing which has nothing to do with aquatic flies or, indeed, with flies of any description in or out of Nature. It is called fly fishing because it is done with the same tools and the same motions, and the lure on the end of the cast is one of those confections of fur, feather, tinsel, hair, and silk.

The fly fisher in the first category, who proceeds on the assumptions set out in my first chapter, is trying to deceive a fish into believing that what he offers it is

actually a living aquatic insect in one or another stage
of its natural development. That is true fly fishing. A
fly fisher in the second category is not trying to persuade a fish that he is offering it an insect. He is trying

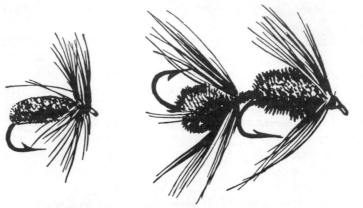

FIG. 3. Hackled Beetle   FIG. 4. Hardy's Worm Fly.
      type of Fly.

to persuade it that his lure represents something else—
generally, a tiny fish, or 'fry'; sometimes, another sort
of organism altogether, such as a shrimp, a beetle, or
even a worm! Since his lure is an artificial confection

FIG. 5. Fresh-water   FIG. 6. Hardy's 'Fly-minnow'.
      Shrimp.

made on a hook, and since he uses a fly rod and fly line
to present it to the fish, we agree to call it fly fishing,
though it ain't. (I hasten to add that it is just as good
fun and just as successful as the other sort of true 'fly'
fishing.)

All salmon flies are of this second kind—they represent, or are said to represent, or are believed to represent, fish fry, or elvers (which are the young of eels), or small marine organisms such as shrimps and prawns. Most sea-trout flies are also within this category.

Herewith Pézare has drawn, just for fun and because they are simply lovely to look at and he likes doing it, a small selection of 'flies' which fall within this category of representations of organisms other than insects. You see, they don't resemble flies at all.

Nevertheless, whether you have on the end of your line a naturalistic or an impressionistic representation of a true aquatic fly in one of its several stages of growth, *or* a thing that looks like a baby eel, *or* something which might possibly pass for a tiny trout or minnow or stickleback—whatever it is, if it is made to deceive, of artificial materials, and plied by means of a fly rod, then you can safely say that you are fly fishing.

I thought we might as well clear this up right away.

CHAPTER 3

What Fish? How Dear?

Just one more thing to clear up before we really get down to cases. What fish can you catch by fly fishing?

I have a notion that there is a fairly widespread idea that fly fishing is a costly, exclusive, and somehow socially 'right' thing to do; that it takes money and inordinate knowledge and skill; and that it is solely a means of catching trout and salmon and other members of the aristocratic family of the salmonidae.

Needless to say, those misconceptions are not current in a country like Scotland, a glorious natural democracy where fly fishing is synonymous with fishing. It is the sort of perversion of the truth which arises naturally enough in a highly stratified money-democracy such as England. It is true that aristocratic anglers have usually been fond of fly fishing, and perhaps rather inclined, regrettably and quite foolishly, to turn up their noses at any other sort of angling. It is true that ninety-five per cent of all fly fishing *is* done for trout and salmon. But all of this is a pity, for it need not be.

The following fish will readily take a fly: salmon; sea trout (known variously as sewin, peal, white trout, slob trout, bull trout, migratory trout, and—at the fishmonger's—salmon trout); brown trout; rainbow trout; grayling; chub; roach; dace; rudd; perch.

The above are fresh-water fish. Of sea fish, the following will more or less readily take a fly: mackerel; bass; mullet; billet; sea trout; herring; garfish; shad.

So unless you are very unfortunate, it is likely that there is water quite near your home containing fish which may be taken by fly fishing. This is true even of waters which have never seen a fly fisher, but which are heavily flogged, weekend after weekend, by maggot-slingers.

I have used the words 'will readily take a fly'. Madness, of course. No fish *readily* takes anything when you are trying to persuade it to do so. What I mean is that they will take a fly just as readily as they will take any other lure or bait. Provided it is presented properly; with regard to which, see the following hundred or so pages, and pray, and endeavour to placate your envious guardian angel, and don't walk under ladders, nor peer at the new moon through glass.

Now about expense. There is nothing inordinately expensive about the fly fisher's gear—at least, there needn't be—but it all depends on what he wants to fish for and where he wants to fish. It is a question of the water, not of the rod and reel and line. If you are content to fish for rudd and dace and chub and so on, then fly fishing will cost you exactly as much as float fishing. If you want to fish for trout and salmon, it depends on where you live. England is rather short of trout rivers, since trout water must be pure, and our history of industrial pollution, which has turned so many noble streams into open sewers, is a sad story. Wales has plenty of trout water, and Scotland abounds in it. Even in England, you can join an association, in most parts, and get a bit of tolerable trout fishing. Or you can save it up for your holidays and have a real go. The same, only more so, is true of salmon fishing.

As in every other walk of life, you get precisely what you pay for. Personally, if I were even poorer than I am, and my fly fishing had to be restricted to a bit of trouting during a holiday, I should press on to the most unregarded and inaccessible moorland or mountain streams. They take a lot of energy and the trout are usually smallish and sometimes inordinately difficult to catch. Therefore they are cheap to fish. (And also, if I may say so, simply fascinating.) That would be my own solution. On the other hand, you can join a club and fish a river which is re-stocked every year from a trout hatchery, and it may cost you anything from a few pounds up to quite fabulous sums of money.

I have been speaking mainly of river fishing. But there has been a tremendous increase recently in the amount of still-water trout fishing that is available—in reservoirs and in private lakes and ponds. It is not very cheap, to put it mildly, but better than no fly fishing at all, even though not everyone enjoys catching big fat stock fish. It has certainly transformed the fly fishing scene.

Well, there is is. Fly fishing is, I believe, the most satisfying and most nearly artistic method of angling. Trout and salmon *are* the queen and king of fresh-water fish. But there are lesser fish to be had on the fly which still provide excellent sport, and fly fishing can be inexpensive.

It can also be ruinous.

But what a wonderful way to be ruined!

CHAPTER 4

The Tools of the Trade: (1) Rods

There are ten fly rods standing in the rod racks around my study walls as I write this. Sometimes the number increases, then I have a nasty bout of conscience and it diminishes. Once in a paroxysm of thrift I took the whole lot down, every rod I owned, and carried them into old Charles Holbrow's little shop in Duke Street, St. James's, and sold them all. A month later I began to build up my collection again. Old friend Holbrow, maker of polo sticks and connoisseur of fishing-rods, has retired now, more's the pity, and London is thereby impoverished.

As I said earlier, this business of the gear is really a matter for your conscience. You can manage on surprisingly little, but there is practically no limit to what you can accumulate—always with a specious 'reason' for buying it. I had better confess right away that I am a bad case of tackle-fever—and an infectious case, too, according to the wives of my friends. I love fishing-tackle and can almost never resist it.

The tools of our trade are beautiful examples of craftsmanship; delicate, responsive, steely, and true. Just to look up from my desk and see them standing around my walls, the rods I have fished with, is to be set free of time and place. That is the rod with which I wandered high tors and moors. That is the wand with which I sauntered down the sunset estuary. With that, I stumbled up the wild glen. With that, I slipped silently down the broad Severn in my canoe. There is not a rod there that has not a story to tell. I glance across at them and the imagination goes free. They are beautiful in their own right, and I love them.

But there is no *reason* to collect tackle, as some men collect *objets d'art*.

Now the indispensable tools of the trade, to a fly fisher, are as follows: a fly rod; a fly reel; a fly line; a gut or nylon leader; a fly.

That is the irreducible minimum. There are countless variations on those five basic ingredients, and there is a whole host of other items which come in very handy. But those five you must have, all of them, and every one of them a specialised tool. You *can* at a pinch make do with a reel that was not designed as a fly reel, but for some other angling purpose. But the rod, the line, the leader, and the fly must be things designed to do a certain job. There is no escaping it. And they must all be considered together, as a harmonious and balanced team which, in use, behaves as one thing.

The FLY ROD is unlike other rods. It has a certain job to do which other rods never have to undertake. A bad fly rod is an abomination. Even a good fly rod is unhappy in the hand unless it is exactly matched by the right reel, line, leader, and fly.

To begin to understand what qualities to look for in a fly rod we must first of all get quite clear in our mind the work which it has to do. Let us have a look at what happens when we cast a fly.

Put your rod up. Fix on the reel, thread the line through the rings, and draw off twelve yards. Lay this line out in front of you—just as it would be lying on the water when you had fished out a cast. (Always practise either on water, which is best, or on grass. Any hard or rough surface gives the line a terrible beating.)

Now you are ready to make a cast. The act of casting falls into two clearly defined, perfectly distinct phases, with a measurable gap between them. First, the back cast. Then, the forward cast.

Pézare's first diagram shows the back cast.

Now this is the most important part of the whole business. I cannot emphasise too strongly that you put all the steam into the back cast—then, if you have your timing right, the forward cast will pretty well look after itself. It sounds a wrong-way-round, para-

doxical way of going about it, since it is the forward
cast which actually delivers the fly. But take it from
me, the back cast governs the whole business.

With a decisive movement, lift the line off the water
(or grass) and fling it behind you. Put it behind you
with real decision. Whether you use only the wrist in
this movement, or the forearm, or the entire arm, or
most of your body, is a matter for dispute among
casters, but I assure you it is of minor importance.

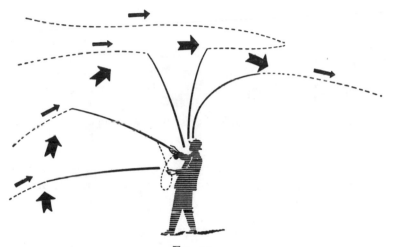

FIG. 7A.

Your stance is your own business: don't be intimidated by anybody's pet ideas. It really doesn't matter
which part of your anatomy comes into play, provided
you put real zip and steam into this motion. If you feel
comfortable, that's right for *you*.

You see that the moment you begin to pick up the
line, the weight of the line begins to put a forward
bend into the rod. Now this is exactly the point at
which you begin to generate the power that will do the
casting. The rod reacts, you see, and bends forward.
The harder you pull up and back, the more the rod
reacts. Now the rod is going to do its best to correct
that bend—*the rod wants to be straight*. Your idea is

to provoke the rod into violent reaction against the distortion which you are forcing on it—and to help it along. You are the instigator of a convulsive reaction against intolerable distortion. You don't aim to throw the line yourself: you aim to talk the rod into doing it for you.

So. You precipitate this crisis in the rod's life by raising it sharply. Having bent forward, the rod straightens, carrying the line up and back. The line streams out behind you.

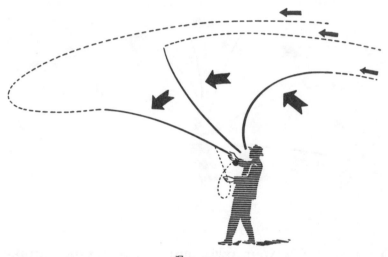

FIG. 7B.

Now a vitally important point: *you stop the rod dead when the butt is vertical in your hand.* This is the crux of the business. You must *not* let the butt flop over backwards. The *top* part of the rod will go over backwards, of course—pulled by the line, and over-reacting against the forward bend which you put into it. That's all right. That's as it should be. But the butt must *never* go back beyond the vertical. If you let it, you take the steam out of the forward motion. You dissipate the stored-up energy in the rod instead of making use of it.

The line streams out behind you, and when there is enough of it behind the rod tip, you will feel a tug. This is the weight of the line pulling the rod tip back. (You see, you miss that if you let the butt drift back behind the vertical.) At this moment, after quite an appreciable pause to let the line go out behind, you start the forward cast.

(If you were casting a short line, you might have to wait until the whole of it was in the air behind you, more or less horizontal, before starting the forward throw. But with a long line you don't have to wait for it *all* to get behind the rod. If you do, it will begin to fall to the ground. The point is that you have to wait until enough line is behind to exert an appreciable pull at the rod tip.)

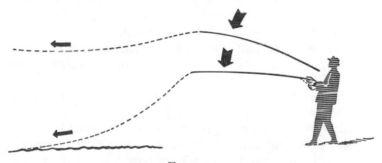

FIG. 7C.

This pull puts a bend into the rod—a backward bend, this time. The rod wants to straighten out again, reacting strongly—and this time it wants to go *forward*, carrying the line with it. It is this intention of the rod which you cunningly aid and abet.

The moment you feel that tug, you snap the rod forward again. The first thing that happens is that your effort increases the backward bend in the rod. It overcomes this, protesting strongly, and the line goes forward.

You stop the forward motion when the rod is at an angle of about forty degrees, the line goes out *over* the

water and you get your distance. When the line is fully
extended you lower the rod point until it is about
parallel with the ground (or water) and you are fishing—your line and fly having fallen neatly on to the
water of their own weight.

As you see, the whole thing is a case of provoking
the rod into reaction against stresses put into it by the
weight of the line plus your own energy. This power to
react is built into the rod, and you must aim to let the
rod work. If you don't—if you try to do all the work
yourself—you might just as well cast with a perfectly
rigid rod; a broom-handle, for instance. That is *why* a
fly rod is pliant.

Don't force it. Rods vary enormously in their power
and their degree of suppleness. You match a rod with
the correct weight of line (see next chapter) and then
all you have to do is initiate the reaction and let it
work itself out. You just help it along.

When making the back cast, think to yourself that
you are throwing the line up into the air—aim it high
behind you.

When making the forward cast, think that you are
aiming the fly at a point a yard *above* the water. Don't
'thrash down'. (In conditions of strong wind, you *do*
thrash down and aim at the water. But that is a refine-
ment you pick up later, when you have got yourself
into the rhythm of casting.)

When you have the hang of it and are making
shortish (not *too* short) casts with ease and fluency,
then is the time to learn to shoot line. This is very
simple. You keep a yard or two of line hanging from
the left hand in a loop. When you have made the forward cast and the line is streaming out nicely, you release this stored line and it feeds smoothly through the
rod rings, pulled out by the line travelling ahead of it.
Nothing to it.

Bring the rod back slightly to one side, and take it
forward again more nearly vertical—i.e. in a slightly
different plane. Thus the rod top describes an ellipse

O—and the line and fly don't hit the rod or get tied up on the forward cast.

Timing is everything. Brute force avails nothing. You put some energy into picking up the line and starting it off on the back cast. Then you take things easily and merely guide the proceedings, helping the rod on at the right moment.

Now I hope that Pézare's drawings, helped or hindered by my words, have partly elucidated the mystery of casting a fly. It is neither easier nor more difficult than riding a bicycle, or swimming. They all three have this in common, that once you have got the knack of it you have it for life.

In learning how to cast you will have picked up, as you went along, a clear idea of what work the rod does and what part the line plays. It must be clear in your mind that the one is complementary to the other. If the line is altogether too light for the rod, it will not make the rod *work*; it will not bring it into action, bring out its latent spring and reaction. If the line is altogether too heavy for the rod, it will kill the rod's action and very quickly break its heart.

A small, light trout rod cannot pick a heavy salmon fly line off the water, much less punch it out against a wind. A powerful fourteen-foot salmon rod will not happily cast a light No. 1 trout line, because the line will not bring the rod's springy power into play. Rod and line *must* match.

Now to cases. First, the choice of a single-handed rod for trout fishing (which also, for our purposes, can be taken to mean sea trout, grayling, roach, rudd, perch, chub, and dace fishing. It is the same general type of single-handed rod which you want in every case).

You will find in the shops an almost infinite variety of single-handed fly rods, and some which are *said* to be single-handed, but which, in fact, need two hands, or the muscular development of an all-in wrestler. You will find limber rods, stiff rods, and rods which fall at every point in between stiff and limber. They will range in price (new) from about £6 to more than £40, in length from six feet to ten feet, and they will be made of split cane or glass fibre.

When I wrote the first edition of this book, in 1958, there was a much wider choice of materials. Rods were still available in split cane, greenheart, and tubular steel, and the glass-fibre rod was only just 'coming in'. Now the situation has changed out of recognition. For one thing, the number of manufacturers has shrunk; for another, greenheart and tubular steel have virtually disappeared, and the proportion of split-cane rods has been drastically reduced. The 'white-hot technological revolution' has swept through the field of fishing tackle, too, and rods made of glass fibre now heavily outnumber rods made of split cane—or any other material.

There is no point in regretting this revolution, though nothing will stop nostalgic reactionaries from doing just that. The new fibre-glass rods are vastly superior to the early models: they have advantages which it would be madness to deny. They are very light, comparatively inexpensive, very nearly indestructible, and can be made to develop surprising power for their weight.

It was inevitable that these plastic rods should come to the fore. Split-cane (or built-cane) rods are made from the hard outer shell of first-quality bamboo, sliced into triangular sections which then have to be glued together, six sections at a time, to form a true tapered hexagon section. For one thing, first-rate bamboo has become increasingly difficult to obtain, the situation in the Far East having developed as it did through the Fifties and Sixties. For another, the fine, meticulous hand craftsmanship required for building and true-ing a split-cane rod has become scarce and expensive. At the same time, glass-fibre technology has been forging ahead brilliantly.

The hollow glass rod consists, basically, of a sort of

'cloth' woven of extruded glass fibres, which is then wrapped around steel mandrels of the appropriate taper, and baked. The mandrels are then withdrawn, and resultant blanks are finished off, and you have a rod which can be reproduced *ad infinitum*, mechanically. Recent developments in phenolic resins, in the almost weightless, non-metallic spigot ferrule, and promised developments in carbon fibres, have all greatly advanced the claims of the good glass-fibre rod as a fishing instrument which will hold its own, or more than hold its own, with a natural cane rod that weighs more and costs a lot more.

All these facts are facts; incontrovertible. Yet there remains a solid core of resistance to the glass-fibre rod. This is purely a question of personal preference. There is certainly a subtle *feel* to a first-quality split-cane rod, which will always attract some anglers who are sensitive to such nuances. I myself greatly enjoy the feel of a good cane rod and shall always use one. But the advantages of the glass-fibre rod are very real, especially on the score of lightness. Not to mention the expense. The early glass rods had a dithery feel which has been eliminated now, and I would certainly recommend a beginner to buy glass fibre for his first rod. As I said, you *can* get one for as little as £6, though a more representative price for a decent tool would be, as I write this in 1976, about £12 or a little less—rising to something more like £22 for a de luxe product. Whereas split-cane rods by the few remaining good makers will run out between about £22 for a brook rod to more than £40 for a pinnacle product.

I think I have to say that the beginner will find a glass-fibre rod perfectly satisfactory and really his best buy. The old hand may prefer split cane, partly from nostalgia, partly for that almost indefinable 'feel' of the natural material. My own collection of 'working' rods includes both sorts, and I would be hard-pressed to rationalise my preference for the timber.

Whichever material you choose, you will be prop-

erly concerned to find an *action* which suits you. Now
the action of a rod is a subtle and arguable thing.
There is no argument that you need a short rod if you
are going to fish small streams, burns, brooks; a longer
rod if you are going to fish wider rivers, or lakes; a
light rod for small trout and a stout rod for salmon.
These things are self-evident. But the mere length and
strength of a rod is not obviously correlated with its
action. The action is the way a rod behaves, the way
it feels in the hand, the way it develops its latent
power.

Built-cane rods can be made to give a stiff action or
a limber, easy action, or an in-between action, at the
whim of the maker. Heat treatment plays a great part
in this; cane is actually 'tempered' almost in the same
way that metal is tempered; but a most important
factor in determining the rod's action is the taper. By
means of various cunningly worked-out tapers you can
have rods of identical length and weight which will
give you entirely different actions. One will bend near
the butt, thereby giving you a relatively slow, easy
action. Another will have a stiff butt and middle
section, and all the action will be concentrated in the
top third of the rod, giving you a very fast 'tip-action'.
Glass-fibre rods vary in just the same way, through
different tapers and variations in the thickness of the
walls of the tubes. But it isn't so easy to get the old
butt action in glass fibre.

Which action do you want? It depends to a great
extent on your temperament and physique. Some
people are brisk, crisp, busy fly fishers. Some are comparatively lethargic—or shall we say easy-going?—in
no great hurry and inclined to regard the whole thing
as mild relaxation. That difference alone will have a
bearing on the rod you choose. But I am probably
the only man who would take this into account or
even admit its existence. All the 'official', technical
reasons for preferring one action to another—perfectly
sound reasons, which I propose to give you now—take

Into account only the purely mechanical and physical considerations.

Such as these. Are you planning to fish mainly with the dry fly—that is, with the fly that is oiled or otherwise treated to float on the surface of the water? Confirmed dry-fly fishers only try to catch fish which they have spotted rising to duns hatching on the surface (or spent flies dying on the surface). They use a floating line. In between casting the fly to fall on the water they make many swishes through the air, which is called *false casting,* in order to shake any water out of the fly and keep it dry. It also helps them to measure the distance and judge the aim.

Now a dry-fly rod, you will already have discerned, needs plenty of backbone and a fairly sharp, steely action. It must be fairly crisp and quick in its action if you are not to waste an inordinate amount of time drying your fly by false casting. It must have guts to stand up to false casting and to punch out a long line accurately against the wind, which is always blowing against you.

Ergo, most experts would tell you that a dry-fly rod must have a firm, fast action, mainly concentrated in the tip, and with a relatively unyielding butt section.

The same experts would tell you solemnly that a rod for wet-fly fishing is an almost radically different proposition. The wet-fly fisher does not want to keep his fly dry. A dry fly is a great nuisance to him. He wants his fly to sink the moment it touches the water— because he is hoping that it represents a tiny fish, or a nymph, and both of these organisms are to be found underwater, not on the surface. Therefore he has to wet his fly thoroughly—in his mouth, as a rule, and it doesn't half hurt when it gets stuck in your tongue or lip—before he makes a cast, and the very last thing he wants is for it to dry out between casts. What he wants most of all is a rod with which he can go on making short casts all day without a trace of fatigue.

It follows that the wet-fly fisher, as a matter of tradi-

tion, prefers a rod with a gentle, easy action. He picks
up the line when he has fished out a cast and flips it
behind him with a gentle, tender movement, and puts
it back in the water first time. No false casting for him.
Therefore a dry-fly rod is wasted on him.

That is a résumé of the usual reasons for choosing
one sort of rod or another. I give it to you because I see
it as my duty to put you in touch with current ideas. I
am not an innovator in this book, but a passer-on of
accumulated reliable lore. However, I cannot resist
telling you that in my private opinion, after years of
fishing, the so-called 'dry-fly rod', stiff, powerful, and
crisp in action, is a perfect abomination. I have sold
my dry-fly models and shall buy no more. Well, not
many.

It is quite true that the stiff, powerful rod will
punch a heavy line out against a wind, and that it has
enough guts to stand up to constant false casting. But
there its virtues end. It makes casting real hard work,
and it makes it all too easy to break fine gut in a heavy
fish.

I am perfectly sure that every beginner would learn
to cast far more easily and happily with a 'soft', wet-fly
style of rod. The limber rod does the work for you. It
imposes its own rhythmic timing on you, and it gives
you far more latitude for making your own errors of
timing. What is more, a gentle rod makes it easier to
hook fish, and *far* less likely that your fine gut will
break in the ensuing struggle. The fact that it will not
cast so far seems to me rather unimportant. 'Distance'
is over-rated. If you cast a very long line you have little
control over your fly.

Two arguments remain. How are you to cast against
a wind? How are you to keep your fly dry? As to the
first, you can usually manage by making a downward
cut at the end of the cast—aiming at the water itself.
Using a size heavier line helps, too. In any case, the
drawback is exaggerated, and I don't find it much
more difficult to send a line 'under the wind' with a

slow-action rod than with a stiff one. As to the second, the false-casting business is very greatly over-rated, and modern silicone floatants will keep a fly water-resistant for hours on end.

You must *always* please yourself. A good rod is costly, and far be it from me to try to impose my personal foibles on you. But I will say this. If offered a stiff rod, grip the butt and see how much sheer energy it takes to make that rod flex merely by tiny, muscular movements of the wrist—almost of the hand alone. If it seems like hard work, try a softer-actioned rod. You will see then how much easier it is to 'bring out the action' of the rod. However, whatever you do, buy the one that feels right in *your* hand. If you are particularly strong, a stiff rod may suit you very well. I can only say that a stiff rod makes fishing hard work for me, and is, by and large, an inefficient fishing-rod.

For a reason which eludes me—if indeed it be a reason, and not merely the rationalisation of convenience in production—makers nowadays seem to have forgotten that there is such a thing as a distinctive action. You can read most catalogues pretty shrewdly without finding a clear definition of a rod's particular action. Virtually no maker now acknowledges that there is such a thing as a 'wet-fly action'. So you will want to find out empirically if a rod has the action that suits you. Fortunately there does still remain a *fairly* wide variation in actions, though the tendency is all towards relative stiffness and quickness. But if you know what you are looking for—and by now, you should—you can go around shaking rods in shops and you will surely detect the differences.

The tendency has been all towards shorter, lighter, stiffer and quicker-actioned rods, in the main, but there has been one countervailing development, the staggered-ferrule rod, which is balm in Gilead to anglers like me who enjoy a butt-actioned rod. The staggered-ferrule rod has a butt noticeably shorter than the top joint—I am speaking of two-piece rods, now—and this does tend to bring the action well down the rod. A nice progressive action—with a shortish length of line out, the flexible top joint does most of the bending; but as the length of line out beyond the tip increases, so the lower or butt portion of the rod comes into play. This is very nice.

I should say that most decent glass-fibre rods are much more 'tolerant' of differing line weights than were their predecessors made of natural wood. This indeed is one of the really formidable advantages of glass-fibre rods. Many of them will work, more or less efficiently, with three weights of line—the 'optimum' weight, the one lighter, and the one heavier. Again, it is a question of the rod's power being brought into action progressively. A light line uses the power of the tip, a heavier line brings out the stored-up power of the butt section. So it is very much easier to 'match' a line to a rod when that rod is glass fibre than ever it was with cane rods.

I may say in passing that most anglers seem to choose too light a line for their rods. This used to have a basis of good sense in the old days—too heavy a line took the heart out of a cane rod quite soon, and it made good sense from the economic point of view, at any rate, to learn to handle a line that was fractionally too light for the rod. With glass fibre, it is almost impossible to break the rod's heart by overloading it, and I should suggest that when the maker gives a choice of line weight, as makers often do—'suit No. 5 or 6 line'—the heavier line will make for easier and more confident casting, at least over medium distances.

Aside from the questions of material and action, there has been another quite significant change in fly rods within the last five years. They have become progressively shorter and lighter. There is little doubt that the trend stems from American usage, primarily, but Continental fly fishermen have strongly abetted it, and now it has reached Britain in full force. It is not an unmixed blessing.

Lightness is a blessing, absolutely. But shortness is not necessarily so. It is a matter of simple mathematics that if a short rod has to develop the same throwing power as a long rod, it must be stiffer. Some very short rods on the market today are much too stiff, in my opinion. A stiff rod can be tiring to use and makes it all too easy to break off fine terminal tackle in strong or heavy fish. A stiff rod also demands a relatively heavy line, to make it work: and a heavy line is a thick line. One should always seek to fish with the smallest possible diameter of line, commensurate with comfortable casting. A thick heavy line makes more disturbance, and throws too wide a shadow, for my liking.

This is not to deny that there is something delightful in going forth equipped with a featherweight little wand—and I know perfectly well that some marvellous fish have been landed on such gear. If it suits your style, so be it. These very short, firm rods call for a technique on its own—they were closely associated, in their origins, with the forward-taper line, virtually a throwing missile, which was originally developed in America. (See next chapter for a dissertation on fly lines.) Using this kind of rod and line, one is not so much casting, in the traditional style, as catapulting the fly out. The technique suits some temperaments very well; it is brisk, busy, and accurate, almost independent of the wind; it enables you to cover a rise with minimum loss of time. To some, this is an appealing technique. Not everyone shares my lethargic, even languorous, preference for the supple throw of a limber rod and thin line.

This essential difference in action and function was quite neatly illustrated by two featherweight rods from the range of rods marketed by that famous old firm, Messrs. Hardy Bros. a little while back. The seven-foot staggered ferrule 'Riccardi' rod weighed three and a half ounces, cast a 6 line, and a strong, crisp 'dry fly' action. The seven-and-a-half-foot 'Jet Set' weighed under three ounces, cast a 5 line, and had a beautiful limber action, entirely different from the other rod. Both, as it happens, cost just about the same. These two delightful little rods posed the choice perfectly: you literally pays your money and takes your choice. The rather longer rod is lighter, slower in action, throws a thinner line: my personal preference every time. But the other rod (no longer in production) will cover a rise fractionally quicker, will perform better against a breeze, and almost certainly will cast a fly rather farther. In practised hands, quite a bit farther.

These short rods really come into their own when one has the opportunity of wading—I have little doubt that they had their origin in wading country, the swift, shallow streams of the Alleghenies and Adirondacks, that sort of territory. They work quite well from dry land when one is fishing small streams, of course, but are quite out of place when fishing wider rivers where wading is either prohibited or dangerous, or for any other reason discouraged. There is a strong school of thought which says that one should never wade where it can possibly be avoided. It is true that careless wading causes very great disturbance and puts fish down wholesale. One should always try to avoid it.

For these reasons, if for no other, I should like to discourage the beginner from buying a very short rod, unless he knows that most of his fishing will be done on very small streams. Often one sees the seven-foot rod described as 'ideal for boys or ladies', but in fact an eight-foot rod weighs so little, in glass fibre, that it is unlikely to tire the slenderest wrist—and its capabilities are so much greater that it may save some frustration.

In the first edition of this volume I recommended a nine-foot glass-fibre rod as ideal for the beginner who was likely to do most of his angling on rivers of fair size, or on lakes and lochs. I still think this is sound advice: it is as near as dammit the perfect choice for the all-rounder, it is light enough for almost everyone to use, its range is wide. With such a rod you can fish for trout, sea trout, and the coarse fish, in rivers and lakes and estuaries. By all means go down to eight feet if you choose, or the increasingly popular length of eight and a half feet. But don't go much shorter than eight or longer than nine unless you have special reasons, of physique or locale, to sway your choice.

There is another material now just coming into production—carbon fibre. Lighter still than glass, and much stronger: an eight-foot rod weighs well under two ounces! And free from dither. Very promising— but unfortunately the cheapest carbon fibre rod (in 1976) happens to cost £56 ...

FIG. 8. Snake (*left*) and Bridge Rings.

Snake rings are the lightest, and adequate. Bridge rings possibly help you to shoot more line. There's very little in it. Reel fittings are unimportant, so long as they will hold a suitable reel quite securely. A suitable reel is one which will hold a suitable line. Press on to Chapter 5.

The Tools of the Trade:
(2) Reels, Lines, and Leaders

Any reel with a check will serve as a fly reel, but reels made specially for the purpose, with a permanent check that cannot be accidentally slipped off, are naturally best. Some are very elaborate, with gradu-

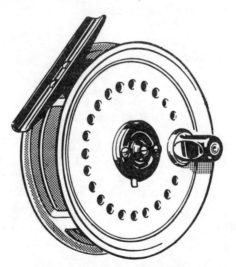

FIG. 9. A typical good fly reel, the Beaudex, made by
J. W. Young & Sons Ltd.

ated brakes and all sorts of gadgets. Though a devoted gadgeteer and a sucker for every sort of tackle advertising, I am happy with the plainest and simplest fly reel. It must hold enough line and backing, run smoothly, and be reliable. That is all it *has* to do. The rest is luxury.

A fly line, on the other hand, is one of the costlier items of the kit, and completely indispensable. There is no substitute for a fly line designed for that specific purpose, and matched to your particular rod.

As you will have learned from the previous chapter, the fly line must be heavy enough to bring out the latent action of your rod, to make it flex and react. (Never forget it is the *line* we are casting—the weightless fly, impossible to cast by any other means, simply travels out with the line, to which it is attached by a length of nylon called the leader.)

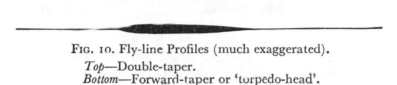

FIG. 10. Fly-line Profiles (much exaggerated).
Top—Double-taper.
Bottom—Forward-taper or 'torpedo-head'.

Length of rod is unimportant, or even actually misleading, when it comes to determining the weight of line to choose. A strong, stiff eight-footer may need a line much heavier than a limber, gentle ten-footer.

Fly lines come in three basic 'profiles': the level line, which is of the same diameter throughout; the double taper line, which is thickest in the middle and tapers off at each end, so that when one end wears it may be reversed; and the forward-taper or 'torpedo-head' line, which really consists of a fine running line with an abrupt thickening near the business end and a sharp, short taper nearest to the fly.

The level line is now not seen so often as it used to be, though it is not only much the cheapest form but also pretty useful. The double-taper line was at one time, when I first wrote this guide, far and away the most popular form, and is still pretty widely chosen. But the forward-taper line, often known by the symbol W.F.—'Weight Forward'—seems to be gaining in popularity. It probably makes it easier to cast a good distance, especially (or principally) when used in conjunction with one of those popular stiff-actioned, lightweight rods. It also goes down on the water with a bit of a wallop, unless you are both careful and lucky. I don't really recommend the forward-taper line for the beginner, who will probably find a double-taper best for all-round angling. The level line works the rod just as well, if not better, but, of course, the taper does help the fly to alight daintily, an important consideration—and it probably helps a bit when shooting line, though I'm not so sure about that.

This weight-forward development has been pushed to its limit in reservoir fishing (see Chapter 14) where distance is all-important for the bank angler. You can buy the line in its most extreme form, when it is appropriately called a 'shooting head'—some thirty feet of line, tapering abruptly towards the fly, which is spliced or attached with a 'nail knot' to many yards of monofilament nylon backing. The technique of casting with these extreme forms of weight-forward lines is quite different from the old-established technique. By vigorously shaking line out through the rings, you 'aerialise' the whole of the actual fly line—usually some thirty feet—and then, while keeping this stout section in the air by false casting, you haul off several yards of the monofilament backing, or running line, with your left hand. When you have what you think is sufficient running line trapped by the left hand, you make your real cast. As the heavy 'torpedo head' or shooting head goes forward, you release the nylon running line, and it feeds up smoothly through the rings of the rod, pulled out by the weight of the fast-travelling shooting head. Prodigious distances may be achieved by this technique. As I have said, it is more like catapulting than casting. It is a reasonably accurate way of throwing the fly a long distance, but it doesn't *feel* like the older method, and unless you are both careful and rather lucky the whole shebang may flop down on the water with more of a splash than I personally care for. But there you are: it's all the rage, it does make distance easy to attain, it does permit the use of strong, light, little rods, it does cheat the wind, it does make fly lines cheaper (a shooting-head line is, after all, only some thirty feet, not thirty yards, of costly stuff). A lot of people actually like this gear; others think it's more like spinning than fly fishing.

As recently as a very few years ago, the fly line most used was made of silk. It was being attacked by lines made of nylon or terylene, but it still held its own. This situation has completely changed, and you may look far and wide without finding an angler using the old-fashioned oil-dressed silk line. The silk line had a very high specific gravity, which made it prone to sink readily but, equally, gave it a small diameter, weight for weight, which made it delightful to cast with. To make it float, one had to anoint it, at fairly regular intervals, with some sort of floatant such as the famous Mucilin, or with mutton fat if you didn't object to that. There were other drawbacks. The oil dressing tended to crack, and when the dressing went the line went soon after. You had not only to grease the line quite often to ensure that it floated well but you had also to be quite meticulous in looking after it when you were not fishing—it had to be cleaned down, dried in the air, and coiled loosely, while not in use, round the back of a chair or in other inconvenient ways. It was a great line, but it did make you work a bit.

Nowadays, virtually all the lines you will be offered in tackle shops are made of plastic. Some are sold with a thin heavy core, even a wire core—for sinking. More are sold with innumerable air bubbles trapped within the plastic, to make them float—for ever, the makers claim. And there are several varieties in between the floater and the sinker. There are floating lines with sinking tips—just the last yard or two sinks. There are slow-sinking lines and there are fast-sinking lines. And in addition to these variations, there are, as I said, different profiles available—level, double-taper, weight-forward, and shooting-head.

It all sounds very jolly. But is it? I don't really think

so. Do you really want to have to buy half a dozen
lines—and perhaps half a dozen reels or reel spools to
store them on—in order to be well equipped to cope
with all conditions that may arise? Some do; some
don't. I will merely point out that the old-fashioned
dressed silk line will perform all the functions, provided you don't mind doing a bit of work (and it
really isn't more laborious than changing over from
one plastic line to another). If you leave it ungreased,
or degrease it with a bit of rag drenched in detergent,
it will sink perfectly. If you grease it all, all of it will
float. If you grease most of it, but degrease the tip, the
tip will sink. You can play all the tunes on the old silk
line. And finally, it has what I personally, with a lifetime's experience behind me, consider a crowning advantage—its high specific gravity and small diameter
cut down wind resistance and make it a nicer line to
cast with, a thinner line on the water, than any plastic
line.

You can still find the old double-taper dressed silk
line, the dear old Kingfisher, though you may have to
ask for it and show the salesman that you mean to
have it. I always mean to have it.

Another big change since I wrote this book has been
in the designation of line weights. This was a much-
needed reform. In the old days lines were rated from
No. 1 to No. 6, but not every maker's rating coincided
with another's. Nowadays, all lines seem to be rated
under the A.F.T.M. system. What this A.F.T.M. number tells you, usually quite precisely, is the weight of
the first thirty feet of line in the air. You don't need to
know what that weight *is*, but you do know that every
rod marked with a given A.F.T.M. number will be
happy with a line of the same number. Actually, the
cumbersome A.F.T.M. is rarely used on rods: instead
we get a symbol, a small double-line cross, like this #.
So #6 on a rod means that you buy a #6 line to
match it. It's a much neater system.

As a matter of interest, roughly speaking, the old No.

1 equals #4, the old No. 2 equals #5, the old No. 3 equals #6, and so on up. Whereas a dozen or so years ago the most commonly used line size for trout rods was No. 2, nowadays it is the equivalent of No. 3—that is, #6. This shows how rods have tended to grow both shorter and stiffer in less than a generation.

One towering advantage of the new plastic lines is that they are highly resistant to corrosion. Maybe they don't *all* float so perfectly and so permanently as the makers fondly believe, or claim, and certainly they are all the better for a wipe down now and again to clean surface scum off. But one thing is indisputable: they are totally unaffected by salt water. This makes them desirable to chaps like me who never miss a chance of doing a bit of fly fishing in estuaries or even in the open sea off the mouths of appropriate rivers which have a run of sea trout or salmon—not to mention the bass that hang about in such locations.

I may seem to have expressed reactionary reservations about the current generation of plastic fly lines. But I freely acknowledge their immense usefulness and convenience; and the best of them, such as the Air Cel Supreme, are beautifully finished and cast well. Some of the cheaper ones are not, and do not.

Between the far end of the fly line and the fly itself comes a short length of nylon which used to be called the cast, and is now more generally called the leader. Another change for the better, in terminology. Since we speak of making a cast with the rod, dreadful confusion used to arise when we also called this terminal bit of line the cast: it is more meaningful to call it the leader, since it leads. An American word, now properly taking over from our native archaism. (You see I'm not reactionary through-and-through . . . Only in spots.)

The first leaders were made of plaited horsehair: 'from a white stallion's tail', for preference. Though less than a hundred years old, I have myself actually fished with a horsehair cast . . . In the latter half of the last century, silkworm gut superseded horsehair, and

retained its primacy until only a few years ago.
Tapered, knotted gut leaders needed careful soaking before use, deteriorated in the light, and had natural
imperfections, as do all natural things. But they were
good to cast with, especially in a wind.

FIG. 11. The Double Blood Knot for joining two strands of
nylon.
(You may easily turn it into a treble or even quadruple blood
knot.)

Now nylon has superseded gut, almost completely.
Early examples of nylon, soon after the last war, were
dreadfully unreliable and earned the material a terrible name. But all that is in the past. Nylon is reliable
enough, now—though you most certainly do have to
learn, and faithfully use, the appropriate nylon knots,
which are lavishly illustrated throughout this chapter.
Learn them well; practise tying them until they become second nature.

If you don't, the day will dawn when you'll regret it.

Nylon is still pretty slippery stuff, even though so greatly improved—you don't want to lose the fish of the day, or the fish of a lifetime, because you couldn't be bothered to learn the double blood knot . . .

FIG. 12. The Blood Bight for forming loop in nylon leader.

It's better if the leader is tapered, so that the change from the thickness of the actual fly line tip, down to the fine bit on which you tie the fly, is gradual. You can indeed 'get away with it', by using just a straight and level piece of nylon cut from the spool; but tapering is attractive for all sorts of logical reasons—it helps

FIG. 13. Forming a Dropper.
(The length of gut left hanging down at right-angles to the main leader is usually about six inches.)

the 'turn over' of the leader in the air, it reduces the mechanical awkwardness of the 'step' down in diameters. If you build up your own leaders from pieces of nylon of decreasing diameter, using the blood knot, you *may* find these knots creating a certain amount of wake or turbulence in the water. I think it's a risk worth taking, except perhaps in very still, smooth water when the light is bright. You can buy leaders (some makers still call them casts) which taper without knots. These used to be fearfully unreliable when they first came out, but I think they are perfectly O.K. now-adays, and often use them.

For many years the 'standard' length of the cast or leader was three yards. I suppose it still is, really. But people fishing clear, still water—reservoir men, for example—sometimes use leaders as long as four yards,

FIG. 14. Figure-of-eight Knot for joining leader to reel line.

and men fishing small streams frequently come down to two yards. If the water is nicely broken, aerated and rushing, use as short a leader as you can get away with —the shorter the better, from the handling point of view. The windier the day, the shorter you want it. But on really glassy water it can hardly be too long— though there is obviously an upper limit imposed on you by the length of your rod. If the leader is much longer than the rod, you can find yourself in difficul-ties, especially when reeling in to land your fish.

FIG. 15. The Turle Knot for attaching fly to leader.

How to land it? A *capacious* net, preferably folding, is probably the best bet. I like to draw the fish ashore, when the configuration of the land makes it possible. But if you are wading, or if the banks are high and steep, then you simply must use a net, and a long-handled one at that. A net is at best a necessary nuis-ance. Secure it to your coat with a cord.

You also need waders *if* wading is permitted and necessary. Rubber-soled thigh boots are all right, unless you have to wade on rocky bottoms; then they are murderous, and you need soles studded with hobs or tackets. You won't need trouser waders unless you are going salmon fishing, and then only in some waters. Gumboots are useful even if you don't wade.

FIG. 16. Priest, for administering last rites.
(*Courtesy Messrs. Milward's.*)

Scissors, a sharp knife, a priest for killing fish, a disgorger for removing hooks, a fly-box (or tobacco tin!), a pair of sharp-nosed pliers, and a bag for carrying fish complete your outfit. Don't overload yourself; it soon takes the fun out of fishing.

CHAPTER 6

Trout

This book tells you something about how to make a start on fly fishing for trout, sea trout, salmon, sea fish, grayling, and the various coarse fish. That is about the lot. But, for most purposes, fly fishing in Britain *is* trout fishing. All the other fish may be angled for with the fly, and very profitably, too. But it is sense to start off with trout, since the vast majority of fly fishing is trout fishing.

The chapters which immediately follow this one, then, are about trout fishing—first in rivers, then in lakes and reservoirs and brooks. Later on, as you will see, I deal with the specific problems of the other fish. But trout fishing is basic. A great deal of what is said in these chapters applies equally well to other sorts of fly fishing.

The brown trout, native to Britain, is fairly widely distributed, though less common in the slow waters of the eastern counties of England than elsewhere. (The rainbow trout, an alien, is not so common, spawns a month later, and fights on top of the water, but is otherwise much the same.)

It spawns in autumn on shallows, preferably gravelly. The hen fish scoops out a depression with her tail and lays her eggs in it. The male fish covers them with his fertilising milt. The season opens again in the spring, when the fish are presumed to have recovered from the gruelling effects of spawning. They may or they may not be fully recovered—it depends partly on the weather, partly on the size of the fish. Big fish take longer to build up their strength again. A bad, cold winter means that there will be little available food in the water, and will delay recovery. In some parts the season opens in March, in others as late as mid-April. Whatever the date, it is too soon. Trout are still ravenous, will take almost anything, and put up a relatively poor fight compared with the battle of the fully recovered fish in late May, say. But there it is.

Brown trout feed avidly after spawning, and again in late summer and early autumn when they are stoking up for the long fast which they undertake when they pair off and head for the spawning beds (which are called redds).

In middle summer they are less eager to feed, less easy to catch.

Trout feed on insects, snails, shrimps, tiny crustaceans, worms. 'Thin', pure rivers running through poor land—such as mountain streams which run over rock—or acidulous rivers which meander through peat, support little life, especially fly life, and therefore breed small, hungry trout. Alkaline waters flowing through limestone or chalk are rich, support huge quantities of insect and other life, and breed fat, relatively lazy trout.

If you fish for trout in chalk stream or limestone rivers, you will find the fish fastidious at times in their choice of fly. Since they have so much food to choose from, they can afford to be fastidious. But if you fish less well-supplied streams you will find trout generally willing to take any sort of fly that is offered to them *in such a manner that they are satisfied it is indeed a living organism.* In between come the many, many waters which are neither very rich nor very poor. These predominate, no doubt about it. In such waters you will usually find that the trout are not too fussy and will take anything that looks to them like a genuine living organism. (Even the most perfect literal imitation, if there were such a thing, which there isn't, would arouse a trout's suspicions if it were not presented properly. 'Properly' means in such a manner that it *behaves* like a living fly.)

I have gone to some trouble to distinguish between

fishing for trout in chalk streams (and limestone rivers, which are similar) and fishing for trout in other, less well-favoured, much more common waters. I do this because I believe that many would-be fly fishers are frightened off the pastime by the complex and forbidding literature that has grown up around it. It is, perhaps, unfortunate that so very much of the literature of fly fishing has been written by men solely accustomed to chalk streams. It is fascinating literature, but unfortunate all the same. The fact is that chalk-stream trout are finicky and exasperating at times, simply because they have such a rich choice of natural food and can on occasion be extremely choosy, taking one particular sort of fly and ignoring all others.

This it is which has given rise to the legend that the fly fisher is a superior being, equipped with great stores of learning, able to distinguish between one fly and another at great distances and to match exactly the fly which the fish happens to be feeding on. He is also credited with superhuman eyesight, 'Superman' skill with rod and line, and a fluent command of Latin technical names. He can cast a fly—exactly *the* right fly, the only one the trout wants—with unerring accuracy on to a precise square inch of water, against a gale, while lying flat on his face in a bed of stinging nettles, murmuring the while a whimsical snatch of Ovid over his shoulder to a respectful and admiring dumb ghillie kneeling one pace to the rear.

This portrait, not *too* far-fetched, is naturally repellent. In fact, chalk-stream angling is a branch apart. Not one of us in ten thousand will ever cast a fly on chalk-stream water. There is so little of it! Most of us will fish less well-blessed streams, less pellucid, certainly less well endowed with fish and fly life. We shall find it utterly delightful—and well within our human capacities. We shall *not* need to learn all the Latin names of flies, nor to recognise at a glance the difference between the male and female spinner of, say, *Ephemerella ignita*. Moderate ability to cast a line—

which improves every time we go out—combined with fair common sense and normal powers of observation, will be all that we shall need. I give you my word.

There is no certainty in fishing, of course; but fly fishing, far from being more difficult than all other branches, is easier than some, and well within the capacity of the normal boy, girl, man, and woman. It is also wholly delightful if you happen to have the temperament for it. Not everybody has. Which is perhaps just as well.

I do not, however, wish to give the impression that it is simply a waste of time to bother to learn anything at all about the natural flies, or the habits of trout. Naturally it increases your pleasure to know as much as you can readily absorb and hold about the creatures which inhabit the water. I give a brief, simple guide to fly recognition and to the distinctly overdone business of matching the natural fly with an artificial (Chapter 15). But for the person who finds that he really cannot absorb or hold all that is to be learned about flies, I bring this comforting news, that on *most* trout waters, an absolute majority in fact, he can catch fish, and catch them quite readily, without knowing one fly from another or one Latin name.

Here is a brief sketch of the trout fisher's year. I offer it because undoubtedly the man who knows what he is supposed to be doing will catch rather more fish and may have more pleasure out of his fishing. But skip it by all means if natural history, even reduced to *my* level of intelligibility, which is pretty elementary, bores or repels you.

In March you may see a big, brownish, upwinged fly—that is to say, a fly which carries its wings almost upright—suddenly hatching in considerable quantities. This will be the celebrated March Brown; the fly I think I love best of all, for in the western waters which I used to haunt it symbolises spring. The hatch never lasts long, but while it does, trout go crazy on it.

(The March Brown is very rare indeed on chalk streams.)

When there is no fly hatching, you can walk the bare river for a mile, peering into bare, weed-free water, and swear there was not a fish in the whole of it. For trout newly recovering from the stress of spawning, though ravenous, hide in deeper, calm holes out of the rush of the current and rise only when there is something to rise to. Their vitality is still low.

April sees the first hatches of the Large Dark Olive. A mild April may also see hatching the Medium Olive —the angler's best friend, perhaps, which will go on hatching throughout the season. On some waters a caddis-fly or sedge-fly called the Grannom will also hatch in quantity. You can always tell it because, like most of the sedge tribe, it does not float placidly on the surface but makes a struggle of it—deeply attractive to the trout, of course. The Black Gnat may also appear in April. The trout's larder is steadily building up.

May, the great month for the fly fisherman—and most of all, perhaps, to the lucky chalk-stream man— brings many Medium Olives, the small Dark Olive, some sedges and Black Gnat—and the great Iron Blue, a tiny, upwinged fly that looks almost black on the water. This is great news: trout and trout fishers love the Iron Blue.

The Pale Watery Dun appears: not that trout are really so mad keen on it, as a rule, but they *do* take it.

You also start to catch fish on spinners in May— spinners being flies that have returned to the water to lay their eggs, and die. You begin to get fun out of the celebrated (often overcelebrated) evening rise.

The Blue-winged Olive appears, an important evening fly, never found in still water. You may also see the Alder, and a day-flying sedge called the Caperer or Welshman's Button. (Most sedges are of nocturnal habit.)

All this time, rises to fly have been of shortish duration. It has not yet been worthwhile getting to the water very early—not before 10 a.m., say. On chalk streams, trout now become a little more inclined to feed at any time of day: long since, on the waters of the West and Wales, trout have been feeding all through the day.

Apart from Mayfly time—mid-May to mid-June, varying in timing and duration, and on many waters entirely non-existent—the months of June, July, and August see the trout less avid, less ravenous. Though in June the important Blue-winged Olive appears on the chalk streams. It is the time to experiment a little —with flies flicked under overhanging trees, for example, where some trout like to lie on the look-out for juicy things dropping from above. The nocturnal sedges are important, and the non-aquatic insect assumes importance for a month or so. Ants fall on the water. You may try the shrimp-fly, the bee, the daddy-long-legs, the caterpillar, the grasshopper. But during high summer you may have to work hard. The trout is not so hungry. He feeds in bursts. He can be very choosy.

FIG. 17. Caterpillar (artificial!).

Come September, the end of the season, trout are feeding steadily again, the water is probably cooler, and flies hatch ever more thickly. The Black Gnat, if he is going to appear at all (he varies year to year), now puts in his big show. Large Dark Olives may appear again, the first time since early spring. The trout get busy, and so do you. There are plenty of spinners. The season almost always ends better than it began.

That is the briefest résumé of the year. For details of the flies, if you want to match the natural with the best artificial, see Chapter 15. For details of how to *fish* them, read on.

CHAPTER 7

Wet Fly or Dry Fly?

A really good wet-fly man is a delight to watch. Size for size and all things considered, I have no hesitation in saying that the habitually successful wet-fly fisher is the most skilful man on the water, anywhere.

A good dry-fly man is also a delight to watch, of course. But let's put it on the line once and for all: dry-fly fishing is beautiful, productive, and deeply satisfying, but it is child's play compared with the subtle and deadly craft of fishing the sunk fly effectively.

True, the well-fished floater will take fish, including big fish; on a good day it will probably lure bigger and better fish than are likely to fall to the indifferently fished sunk fly. But good days are few and far between: that is one axiom on which I do not fear to be challenged. And it is on the *average* day that the skilful wet-fly fisher will take fish while the average dry-fly addict will not.

Put another way, the dry-fly man will catch fish when they are obviously feeding (on floating flies). The expert wet-fly man will take fish (if they are at all takable) when they are *not obviously* feeding on anything at all. Surely the advantages of learning to fish the sunk fly well are sufficiently obvious? But it is a tiny minority of fly fishers who bother to master the craft.

Thinking back to first principles for a moment: the fly spends by far the greater part of its life under water. Ergo, it is by far likelier to be eaten by fish while it is underwater. The reasoning is elementary and irresistible.

The time the dun or hatched fly spends on the surface of the water is infinitesimal compared with the

time it spends underwater, as a nymph. In fact, a fish
has to be fairly smart, and energetic, to secure a
hatched dun: whereas a fish has plenty of time to
secure nymphs, at all stages in their development,
without putting himself to the trouble of rising to the
surface and poking his nose out into what is, after all,
an alien element. To a fish, the act of *rising* to a fly is
something like a *dive* would be to us: quite a business,
extracting energy and involving a brief contact with a
deadly element in which it could not survive.

FIG. 18. Three typical nymphs.

No wonder, then, that it has been calculated by
better men than me that a trout does at least ninety
per cent of its feeding underwater—i.e. without rising
to the surface. So the dry-fly purist deliberately sacri-
fices ninety per cent of his chances of catching a fish.
All honour to him, and the best of luck. But if you
want a better than one-in-ten chance of interesting a
fish you will learn to fish the sunken fly well. We aren't
all altruists.

There is yet another excellent reason for learning
the difficult craft of wet-fly fishing. It is this. We have
said that when fish are rising to a hatch of flies the
good dry-fly man will catch them. True. But in those
same circumstances *the wet-fly fisher will catch them
too*. Fish very frequently concentrate on underwater
flies (i.e. larvae and nymphs) to the exclusion of
floaters. Often and often, as every dry-fly purist has
discovered to his bafflement, fish will ignore floating
flies even when they are hatching in numbers. Such fish
are often feeding adequately on the nymphs and will
not trouble to take the more difficult floaters. *But* the

converse is rarely, if ever, true. Whenever fish are rising to the floating fly they will also fall for the sunk
fly—naturally, the sunk fly fished very shallow; for,
admittedly, their attention is then concentrated on the
upper or surface layer of the water. However, the fact
remains that fish which are not rising may frequently
be taken with a sunk fly, and fish which *are* rising may
also frequently be taken with a sunk fly: whereas fish
which are not rising cannot be taken on a floating fly
(save in exceptional circumstances, which will be dealt
with later).

It all seems to add up, I think, to a powerful argument for learning to fish the sunk fly well. And there is
one further argument yet. The wet-fly fisher is not confined to using representations of aquatic insects. There
are many carnivorous or cannibalistic fish which have
no interest, or only a slight interest, in insects: most
fish are *sometimes* within this category. To the dry-fly
purist, such fish are entirely out of reach. The wet-fly
man, on the other hand, can tempt them with subtle
representations of other food than insects. Using his fly
rod and fly line, and behaving in every respect as a fly
fisher, he can offer them simulacra of fish fry, minnows,
shrimps, beetles, and other dainties.

In fact, it boils down to this. The dry-fly purist
places himself deliberately at a disadvantage. The all-
rounder who can handle dry and wet fly with equal
aplomb is very much less likely to find the blank days
in his diary outnumbering the red-letter days.

I make no recommendation in any *ethical* sense.
How absurd that would be. If you want to restrict
yourself to the use of the dry fly you will find yourself
in very good company. On very many waters you will
find that the regulations *oblige* you to use no fly but
the floater. So be it. My purpose here is simply to
acquaint you with all known methods of fly fishing. I
am not very likely to change my private view—that
wet-fly fishing is the most highly-skilled, most profit-

able, and perhaps the most fascinating of all angling exercises. Certainly the well-equipped fly fisher should understand what is involved in it. So let us proceed on that assumption.

CHAPTER 8

Wet Fly: The Elements

It helps to know what you're *supposed* to be doing. Nothing knocks the shine off fishing faster than blindly following some mechanical routine without understanding what the underlying reason is for the motions you're going through. Yet thousands of fishermen do just that, day after day, year after year. Fly fishermen in particular. 'Coarse' or bait fishers seem to understand their craft rather better, on the whole. They are a bit nearer to the fundamental, earthy, organic truths of angling, and less inclined, perhaps, to slavish snobberies.

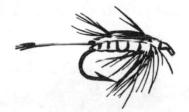

FIG. 19. Nymph (Pheasant Tail).

When you are wet-fly fishing you are doing one of two things. You can't possibly be doing both at once. *Either*

(1) You are trying to present to the fish an imitation of a nymph, which is an embryo fly struggling to reach the surface and hatch out,

or

(2) You are trying to present to the fish an imitation of a tiny fish, a fry.

If (1), then you have to simulate the behaviour of a nymph. If (2), then you must simulate the behaviour of a tiny fish.

Behaviour is almost everything. It's no good buying or tying a perfect (!) representation of a nymph and then undoing your good work by making it behave in the water as a fish fry behaves. It's no good tying on a plausible representation of a fish fry and then making it behave like a nymph.

Fish aren't *that* stupid. They aren't very clever, but they've seen nymphs and they've seen fish fry. The thing you have tied on the point of your cast isn't a very brilliant imitation, anyway—the best in the world isn't very good, it comes nowhere near the natural thing in translucency, gossamer texture, *life*. Nowhere near. How *can* it when, for a start, you have a whacking great iron hook running through the middle of it and dangling down in a sinister curve with a barb on the end? The best imitation in the world is a rude and primitive shot in the dark.

FIG. 20. Hardy's Midget Spinner.

All you can do is get the fly about the right size, and as subtly tied as may be—and then *give it life*. Far more important than precise imitation of the way the creature is *made* is precise imitation of the way the creature *behaves* in the water.

It's an illusionist you are.

Now, how does a nymph behave? It wavers and wanders, trying to swim up to the surface, but often drifting down towards the river-bed. Its general course, like a graph, is plotted upwards—with downward sags; but all the time it struggles towards the surface it is being carried downstream by the current. Against which it is perfectly powerless to fight.

So. If you are trying to represent the nymph, you must cast upstream and let your artificial nymph drift down with the current.

But if you are trying to simulate a tiny fish, then you want to make your lure behave as a fish fry behaves. And how is that? Well, it swims, it has independent mobility. It isn't very strong, but it can swim against the current, to some extent. Moreover, being fishy, it prefers always to lie with its head pointing upstream.

So if you toss a fry lure in upstream it will drift down quite unnaturally, lifelessly, looking like nothing that inhabits the stream. But if you cast in your fry lure downstream and hold it taut at the end of your line, the current working upon it will keep it 'lying with its head pointing upstream'; and if you cause it to move through the water against the current, *at a realistic speed*, you will basically be doing the right thing—i.e. representing the behaviour of a fish.

So, you see, there are two entirely different methods of wet-fly fishing. So different, they are as unlike as wet-fly and dry-fly fishing. The only thing they have in common is that the fly is sunk beneath the surface.

Yet how often do you see an angler with a 'team' of flies on his cast, including a nymph and a flasher, or attractor? You see it very often. It doesn't matter how he fishes such a so-called 'team'—*one* of his flies must be wasted. If he casts it downstream and holds it against the current, the flasher is behaving right, but the nymph is behaving absurdly. No nymph can swim strongly against the current. If he casts it upstream and lets it drift down, the nymph may be behaving well, but the flasher is wasted. *Fish* don't drift inertly down the water. If they did they'd *drown*. (Oh yes. If you pull a fish down the stream, or hold a fish with his head facing downstream, he will drown. He depends on the movement of water over his gills—in at the front, out at the back—for his oxygen, his breathing.)

As you have gathered, the first thing is to decide whether you are going to fish the flasher, which imitates a small fish, or the nymph, which imitates a nymph. You can't mix your methods.

Let us start with the oldest form of fly fishing—the use of the 'fish' lure, cast across and down the stream.

CHAPTER 9

Across and Downstream

This is certainly the most old-fashioned form of fly fishing; the original, perhaps. I guess so. Dry-fly fishing is a modern invention—it became popular only in the nineteenth century. True nymph fishing is a twentieth-century invention. In the real old days fly fishing meant fishing an attractor downstream.

In fact, there is very little difference, if any, between this kind of fishing and spinning. Except for the gear you use, there is *no* difference. For what are you trying to do? You are trying to convince a fish that here at the end of your line is a tiny, succulent morsel of fish-life—*in trouble*. A bit of a slip of a fry, struggling to maintain itself against the current. Easy meat, in fact, for a predator. That is exactly what the spinner sets out to do, with his spinning reel and his Devon minnow or spoon.

So let's not be too superior about the spinner. I must say I love a bit of spinning. It has got a bit of a bad name for two reasons: (1) some pukka fly fishers can't spin; (2) some good spinners catch too many fish.

That's all there is to it.

Well, now, you are going to have a shot at the good old downstream, or what used to be called 'across and downstream', method of wet-fly fishing. The best of luck. You'll be drummed out of your club if it is a pukka chalk-stream association. On the other hand, you may possibly be well out of it.

Come with me, now, to some remote and splendid part of the country that hasn't been priced out of everybody's reach save wealthy stockbrokers'. Here we are among the eternal hills, and we'll just light a fire of twigs and brew up before we start fishing.

Around these parts you'll see ravens and buzzards, but few human vultures. That river runs as it has run since the crust of the old earth cooled and shrank with magnificent great steamy detonations. No syndicate of superior persons elaborate absurd rules to govern your conduct upon it. You will be guided by your innate sense of what is fit. You will not poach other men's fish and you will not so work, with stout hawsers, grapnels, sniggles, gaffs, and throw-nets, that no fish can escape your greed.

No, indeed; you will fish like a sportsman, giving the fish a fair chance—but all the same, you will fish to kill and you will use whatever method of fishing the fly strikes you as appropriate and profitable. For, God save us all, you have come all this way in order to catch fish, and catch them you shall.

Put up your rod, then, your limber, easy-actioned, honest rod. Anoint those ferrules with a film of good oil before you put the rod together—simply by rubbing them in the hair at the back of your neck. What a fool you look while you're doing it. Who cares? There's none here to see but me, laddie, and I'd far rather watch a man rubbing a ferrule on the back of his neck than a man writing in a ledger or using a telephone or speaking on television.

Stick the reel on the rod. If your rod is costly it will probably boast complicated screw-winch fittings, made of polished duralumin, which look fine and do a superbly efficient job. If not, and you have to make do with simple sliding rings, it may pay you to take a turn of adhesive tape round the reel seat. I always do.

Thread the line through the rings. No need to fiddle around with greasing it. It's meant to sink, in this exciting business we're engaged on now. True, you must remember to give it plenty of fresh air when the fishing's over. You must always strip the line off the reel and wind it on to a line winder—or round the back of a chair—to let the air circulate and dry it. Leave it coiled on the reel, wet, and it won't last six seasons. Take care of it, dry it, air it, wipe it down, wax it, polish it between your fingers with a soft cloth, keep it stored on a winder—and it will last a lifetime, very near. I've seen fly lines thirty years old, so help me, and as supple as the day they left the maker. No, suppler. Good fly lines improve with careful use. They deteriorate with frightening speed if abused. (Though the new plastic ones (Chapter 5) last longer.)

Now tie on your leader with the figure-of-eight knot or some other you trust better. For some work, I prefer a true gut leader. When you have to cast with real precision—perhaps against or across a wind—then true silkworm gut is unbeatable. It goes out steely and straight. But for this light-hearted downstream business, the current catches the leader and straightens it as soon as it hits the water, and there's no need for pinpoint accuracy. So nylon will do perfectly well, and at a fraction the cost. Your leader should be three yards long, if not a foot longer. Never less than the good old nine feet regular. You want to keep that thick fly line a secret from the fish. You want to put the maximum possible distance between fly and fly line. As much of the gossamer deceitful stuff as you can handle should be between them. Trout are scarey creatures.

How thick, how thin? Well, on this sort of mountain stream, this wild, remote river, we'll not be expecting the trout to run to monster weights, and 4X is amply strong for all we'll need. I have landed trout up to three and a half pounds on 4X. Better men have landed salmon on 3X, and I wouldn't mind having a shot at it myself, if the luck was with me. So 4X for the point—that is the part of the leader nearest to the fly.

Level or tapered? I always advise the tapered leader. It helps you to make a better job of casting, it helps to let the whole machinery of line-plus-leader straighten out nicely and go down sweet and straight on the water. You can see why: an abrupt step down in diameter between fly line and leader is a sort of sharp hinge. The line goes out, but it doesn't carry the leader with it so suently, as they say in the West Country. So sweetly. So I like a leader with a thick butt end, not much thinner than the end of your fly line. Tapering down, step by step, to that 4X point. Since we are dealing with nylon in this form of fishing, it is extravagant to buy ready-made leaders. We build our own, buying spools of nylon of varying thicknesses and making enough leaders out of them to see us through our finest years, at negligible cost.

Mark you, they make knotless tapered nylon leaders, these wonderful days, and there is nothing to touch them, if you care to lash out the money. Obviously, every knot in a leader tends to show up and/or cause a faint disturbance in the water; which is bad. Knots often collect tiny air bubbles, which is also bad. The knotless tapered leader cuts this out. On the other hand, we are going to need droppers on which to tie some of our multiple team of flies, and the sound spot to tie in a dropper (see Pézare's sketch in Chapter 4, page 45) is a blood knot joining two sections of the leader. So there's a very great deal to be said for building up our own leaders. In fact, I always do.

How many flies? Most expert downstream wet-fly fishers would say three, I think. On a really brisk stream, three, then. But on a calm stream, two is plenty. Three looks a shade suspicious, I think, when the water is calm enough for the fish to have a good look at them. There's altogether too prominent a network of nylon to arouse their easily aroused suspicions.

Here it's rough and rapid, as I love it best. Call it three if you feel like it. I have gradually formed the habit of never using more than two, so you tie on three and I'll content myself with two and we'll see how it goes.

What flies? Well, there's no sign of a fly on the water. You mustn't expect it. This is thin, rocky water, not given to nurturing flies. What we are going to mount is a team of representations of fish fry, re-member.

At the tail, then, the so-called point, the ultimate extremity of your leader—a Butcher. Glorious, murderous, brutal, hard-working Butcher. How many fish have I slain with your aid! The greatest of all the unequivocal attractor flies. In all its several variations —and I know of at least five versions of the Butcher— it remains the same thing: a convincing representation, by no means unduly surrealistic, of a small fish such as a minnow or the fry of trout. The silver gives off flash, the sheen of that deadly blue-black wing is fishy, the red hackles and whisk suggest, oh so strongly, fins and blood. On the point, now and for ever, a Butcher.

Choose which you will. Simple and splendid Butcher, Bloody Butcher, Gold-bodied Butcher, Hackled Butcher, Blue Butcher. It matters not. Let butchery be afoot.

Next to the Butcher, eighteen inches nearer the rod, tie the second truly great wet fly. A March Brown.* All the season round a friend of mine fishes the March Brown. Such austerity is beyond me: I enjoy the severality, the variousness, the rainbow splendour of the fly box. I lack the iron self-denial to follow him. But he is right! He catches numerous fish! The March Brown, subtler than the blatant Butcher, subtly fishlike in action: the silver-bodied March Brown, that is your second fly, and there is no arguing the matter.

For your top fly—ah, but here disputation raises its vile yet nourishing nob. *What* is your top fly to represent? What do you plan for it? Is it to be sunk as the others, yet another attractor? Or is it to be a true *bob fly*, a true dapper on the surface, to be drawn lightly across the water, simulating a veritable insect, while the others work for you, fish-like, below the surface?

You must make up your mind. If you are fishing the team fairly shallow, you may well simulate a hatching fly by making your bob fly dance upon the surface. It is deadly attractive. In that case, make it a proper insect: say, a March Brown, hackle-tied, to float; or a

Greenwell's Glory, which, praise the old Canon, simulates effectively most of the Olive tribe. Or a Gold-ribbed Hare's Ear, the fourth immortal fly that I have mentioned in this chapter.

But if you are going to fish deepish, and if you doubt that the fish of this thin stream are much given to looking up towards the surface in the expectation of taking floating flies—then, logically, my logical mannie, you will make yet a third attractor do the job. A Zulu is undoubtedly the smartest bet for the job— for a Zulu, though it looks effective under water, also works tolerably well as a bob fly when, at the end of the cast, you draw your flies towards the surface. I would always choose a Zulu for this function. But you have the choice of many tried attractors: Peter Ross, Black Spider, Teal-and-Green, Teal-and-Red, Mallard-and-Claret, Invicta, or the gaudy minnow called, by courtesy, a fly, and surnamed the Alexandra. But let's chance our luck with the Zulu.

Now you are ready to fish, with your Butcher, your silver-bodied March Brown, and your Zulu. I am at your elbow, eager for your success.

* POSTSCRIPT. Yes, there *is* a real fly called the March Brown, and there is, of course, a representation of the March Brown nymph. But it remains true that the wet or sunk March Brown, especially the silver-bodied version, works very well as an attractor, simulating fish fry or who-knows-what?

CHAPTER 10

Fish Gotta Swim

One of the most agreeable reflections on this branch of fly fishing is that the lure works harder than in any other branch, but the angler does practically no work at all. It is the nearest known instance to 'something for nothing' in fly fishing.

Certainly there is no sense in making your pastime hard work. True, some city types are so soft, they lead such silly lives, that if they didn't get exercise at their pastime they would soon be in the box. But if you are moderately well, there is no point, so far as I know, in whacking yourself deadbeat at your hobby.

All fly fishing is more strenuous than any other form of fishing. You accept that at the start. But the least demanding form of fly fishing is this caper on which we are now embarked. For in this aspect of the game, we make the water do the work.

This river on whose banks we find ourselves is a lucky one, like all rivers in books. Although the far side is steep, on our side there is nothing behind us to hamper the back cast. So there is no need to wade and no need to employ the specialised switch casts, which are really very easy but look rather difficult and tend to put people off.

It is lovely to wade—I am passionately fond of it— but in fact it is simply a sensual pleasure and should be sternly avoided wherever possible, in the interests of good fishing. There *are* occasions when you simply must wade to get to your fish. But, as a general rule, let's observe it as a dictum: *Never wade unless you must.* For, obviously, a man clumping around in the water, stamping and sliding and slipping on rocks, stirring up mud, sending huge bow waves ahead of him—such a man is not observing the fundamental principle of all angling, which was laid down by old Izaak long ago: *Study to be quiet*. If you have to wade, learn how to do it as silently, slowly, and inconspicuously as possible. It is quite difficult and well worthwhile to master the craft.

But here we have no problems, we have bags of room for the back-cast, the river is not so wide that we can't reach across to the far bank with a goodish long cast. There is simply no point in entering (and disturbing) the water.

Even if it were a wide river, we ought to begin by casting from dry land, first covering the water nearest to our bank. I know that there is, always and everywhere, an irresistible inclination to believe that the most desirable fish are on the other side. That is simple human nature, a neat combination of naïvety and greed. But if you only try to remember that the chap on the opposite side feels exactly the same about *your* bank, it will help to assuage the mad urge to start casting the longest possible line right away.

Generalising in the wildest way, I should say that in most rivers most trout lie nearer to the bank than to the centre of the stream. Therefore, if you plunge right in, or if you start lashing your line down on the nearer two-thirds of the water in a passionate attempt to reach distant fish, you stand a first-rate chance of scaring all the fish which *do* lie right in near to your own bank. Do try to remember this. Scared fish communicate their alarm.

It is, then, good sense to start casting with a very short line, covering the water right in to your own bank. In fact, it is prudent to make your first casts while standing well away from the water. If it is a small river you should *never* get right to its brink. Use the 'overland' cast, which explains itself—just an ordinary cast, but made from so far back that, while you remain unseen and unsuspected, some part of your line actually falls on the ground and only the terminal part of it on the water.

(This you can do only if the shore is level, or very gently sloping into the water. If the water is down deep in a sort of canyon, you won't be able to see your end tackle and you will have no idea what is happening to your fly.)

These first overland casts, just one or two, gradually lengthening line, are merely try-outs, little more than pious offerings, gestures, made to the pagan god of the wilds who awards trophies to the subtle one who moves with stealth. Unless a fish grabs your fly very determinedly—but, mark you, a fish sometimes *will*— you feel no reaction and you assume correctly that there is nothing doing just under your own bank. Stealthily, then, having heard no splashy rise and felt no thrilling pluck, approach the water and prepare to fish it out from the water's edge. Or near enough.

Your first cast should be a moderate one as to length —on a smallish river such as we are fishing, and such as most of us fish most of our lives, it should be aimed at about the middle of the river, and angled very slightly downstream. Very slightly. The moment your line falls on the water you drop the point of your rod until it is almost touching the water. The current now seizes your line, and swings it in towards your own bank. Where the line goeth, there go your leader and your flies. They have no option. They swing across the current, at first almost broadside on, but at a swiftly diminishing angle to the current, until the line lies straight downstream under your own bank.

Follow it round reluctantly with the rod tip. Don't lead it, or you will momentarily ease the tension of the current and lose touch with your flies. As it swings round, gently raise and lower your rod tip, about a foot of movement each way, up and down. This will help to give your flies a darting, fluttering motion in the water. Never forget that they are supposed to simulate tiny fish, struggling in the current.

As soon as the line lies straight under your own bank, start to twitch the flies upstream towards you.

This you do by pulling the line through the rod rings. A normal right-handed angler uses his left hand to retrieve line. The right hand is holding the butt of the rod. Trap the line loosely under the forefinger of this hand, putting a slight pressure on it. With the left hand, draw in the line with minute tugs, taking about two inches of line at each tug, and spacing the tugs about two seconds apart.

So your flies will struggle back towards you. Don't overdo it. A tiny fry can't battle a current with much success. He's doing well to hold his place against it, and big fish know this. But it's just that desperate litle *darting* motion which so often brings the predator to life.

I think it is a mistake to spend too long on this retrieve. If you pull in all your line, you have the job of getting it all out again by false casting, which is not only a nuisance but also dries off your flies so that they sink reluctantly on the next cast. (Always you will find the first cast or two unsatisfactory, for until the flies and leader and line are thoroughly soaked they will not sink readily. It is a cardinal point with the wet-fly man to secure *rapid penetration* of his flies. To help towards ensuring this, he soaks both leader and flies thoroughly before he starts to fish.)

You have done your duty. You have approached the problem with a hunter's stealth and patience. You have made your propitiatory preliminary casts—and how few anglers bother to do so—your overland and your halfway starting cast. They have not rewarded you positively today—one day they *will*, never doubt it—but, all the same, they have brought you a considerable, if unseen and as yet intangible, reward. You've started right by not scaring away any fish which might have been lying, unseen, near your own bank. Now you can boldly start the fishing proper, the excellent rhythmic exercise, so splendid and soothing, of the full-length regulation cast.

How long is full-length? It depends partly on you,

partly on your equipment, and partly on the river. On this little river which we are fishing, you with your nine-foot rod and light line can just about reach the other bank and a yard to spare without killing either yourself or your wand. Call it fifteen yards? Perhaps no more than a dozen. It couldn't be better. Hereafter you will aim every cast to fall a foot or so short of the opposite bank.

Take your first. Lengthen line. Easy and rhythmical. Unhurried. Unforced. Good. Now let it go. *Swish* it sings through the air, landing in the water near the far bank and about ten degrees (a couple of yards, perhaps) downstream of where you stand.

You fish out this cast exactly as you did the previous one. Whereas the previous cast covered a smaller arc and searched the water within a radius of about ten or a dozen yards, this one is searching the entire river within an arc of perhaps fifteen yards or so—perhaps a bit more, perhaps even less; but, anyway, a nice easy average cast.

When you have fished out the cast you step downstream and cast again. As you proceed, your flies search practically the whole of the water. What distance you should put between each cast is a matter of considerable disputation among anglers. Some favour slow fishing, searching the water meticulously, moving no more than a good yard between casts. Others incline to quick fishing, stepping down two or three or even four yards between every cast.

I incline to the view that in this particular business it pays to fish briskly and cover a lot of water. When I am fishing the nymph upstream—an exacting and highly profitable craft to which we turn our attention in the next chapter—then I am a very slow fisherman. I wouldn't mind spending half a day on a two-hundred-yard stretch, if it were a good one. I should expect to finish up with more fish than a man who is constantly rushing up the river, flicking a fly in here and then panting off to find a more profitable piece of water elsewhere. But in the across-and-down style of fishing I think different considerations apply. After all, your team of flies swings through a very wide arc of river, and fish have exceedingly sharp eyesight. At least, though ichthyologists may disagree about the nature of their vision, you and I had better assume that there is nothing wrong with it. Indeed, I am convinced that fish see a flasher fly a long way off. They may not move to it, but they see it.

So on the whole, I think it is better, when you are fishing across and downstream, to cover a good deal of ground. Fish the actual cast out slowly and carefully, concentrating every second. But when it is fished out, you can take it for granted that every fish within a wide radius has had a fair chance of seeing your flies. It is bad policy to move downstream one pace and repeat the whole business, for fish which haven't accepted your first offer will only be made even more suspicious if they see this team of flies travelling across the water yet again. Make a bold break, move downstream three yards at least, four if you like, and cast again. Then you stand a chance of interesting a whole new lot of fish.

By the time you have taken half a dozen casts, or even fewer if your preparations have been shrewd and careful, your line will be sinking nicely and your flies fishing as well as they are ever likely to fish, well down in the water. Now what about catching some fish?

Well, if you have anything like halfway decent luck, you will sooner or later feel a thrilling little pluck at your line. Instantly strike, quite fast and sharp—though not, of course, so coarsely and brutally that you run a chance of smashing your leader. Sometimes fish will hook themselves; more often, you need to give a twitch to help the business on. I should describe this business of striking as a half-hearted sort of back cast. Just raise the point of the rod and throw the line up in the air as if you were about to make a new cast but hadn't really made up your mind.

At times you will actually see a flash underwater as a fish turns with your fly. Sometimes you will see a bulge in the water, sometimes your line will just stop. Any of these things means that a fish is taking one of your flies. But with the line stretched pretty taut, the usual sign will be a sharp, slight, indescribably thrilling little tug.

You will miss many fish. It is not a highly efficient fishing method from the point of view of *hooking*, since the tendency is to pull the fly straight out of the fish's mouth. But it is very efficient from the point of view of attracting fish.

If you catch two or more fish and find that they have all taken one particular fly of your team of three, then it would be mere common sense to change the cast and use a team consisting exclusively of that fly. There *are* times when fish will concentrate exclusively on one particular sort of fly. In lake and loch fishing this happens fairly often. But in your downstream river fishing I shouldn't expect it, as a general thing. One flasher is pretty well as good as another.

I must add a rider about greasing the line. Some very good wet-fly fishers grease their lines, excepting the last yard or two. Others, equally successful, don't grease it at all. I hardly know what to advise. I think it must largely depend on the water. Obviously, if you are fishing fairly deep water and have to get your flies down well, you must not grease the line. If you are fishing shallow water—say, up to four feet deep—the flies will get down far enough even with a floating line: always provided that the last yard or two of it does *not* float.

But there is yet another point to bear in mind. A floating line casts a deadly great shadow on the bottom of the river. A sunken line casts nowhere near so formidable a shadow. Test this for yourself by experimenting, in a bath or a water butt. The sunk line throws a shadow, of course, but it is much diffused and broken up. This is a telling reason, with me, for not greasing the line.

On the other hand, a greased line, floating, is very much easier to pick neatly off the water when the time comes for the next cast—and it makes life much easier for the rod. I really would not care to dogmatise about this: you have heard the arguments for and against and must make up your own mind. Bear in mind all the factors, including the terrible strain which is put on a light rod when it has to haul a sunken line out of the water thousands of times.

Before passing on to upstream wet-fly fishing, I want to make it clear that I have deliberately started you off with this old downstream style *not* because it is the 'best' method, but because it is the easiest and therefore the best *for a beginner*. Other methods are perhaps more intelligent and efficient; we are coming to them. But the downstream method is the most encouraging for a beginner, and I want you to get confidence as soon as possible. The current corrects faulty casting, no great accuracy is needed, and you get into the fluent rhythm of fly fishing more quickly and comfortably. When you have caught a few fish in this delightfully self-indulgent manner, then is the time to aspire to the real craft of the upstream wet fly. Here goes.

CHAPTER 11

Upstream Wet-fly and Nymph Fishing

Now, although we are still dealing with wet-fly fishing, you must forget everything I wrote in the previous chapter and start afresh. For the difference between downstream wet-fly fishing and upstream wet-fly fishing is radical. They are entirely different methods, and the reasoning behind the techniques is based on entirely different approaches.

Fishing the wet fly downstream we were presenting to the fish a simulacrum of a tiny fish—something which might well, in nature, struggle to hold its place against the flow, and even to buck the current. Fishing the wet fly upstream, we are entirely concerned with

FIG. 21. Nymphs—Pheasant Tail and Tup.

presenting to the fish a true nymph. We are genuinely *fly* fishing. We are offering the fish an aquatic insect in an early, or pre-hatch, stage of its development. All that we do is governed by this assumption.

Now how does a nymph behave? When it starts its progress towards the surface, swimming hard, it makes a very erratic job of it. Sometimes it rises in the world, sometimes it goes down. Its progress is like a sales chart, or a graph of the pound's stability. But *always*, whether it is rising towards the surface or sinking momentarily towards the bottom, it is being carried slowly downstream by the current.

For a nymph is a feeble thing.

So how do you go about the task of imitating a hatching nymph? First, of course, you tie on an imitation which looks something like the natural thing. Secondly, you make it behave in the water as the natural thing behaves. The two desiderata which govern all fly fishing and can never be dodged.

As for imitating the natural nymph, well, this is not a book on fly tying, and you are assumed to be buying your flies from a tackle shop or a fly dresser. There is plenty of choice. Not very long ago it was the most difficult thing to obtain good imitations of the nymph, but fly dressing has made great strides, even since the Second World War, and nowadays you will have no difficulty in buying first-rate nymphs. You can also buy weighted nymphs which sink readily, and in certain circumstances they are much to be desired.

In addition to the modern nymph, so-called and properly so-called, there is the vast range of old-fashioned 'wet flies' which are, in fact, nymphs, though quite crude ones. Now some of these are still extremely useful. The old wet fly, as you know, is divided into fishy flashers, or attractors, and representative imitations of true insects. Some of these latter were and are quite good nymphs. The old tendency to overdress such flies with festoons of hackle is a little less noticeable nowadays, I think, under the influence of the new true-nymph school. Certainly many of the old wet flies, sparsely dressed, with a mere wisp of hackle, make excellent nymphs.

The 'spider' school of dressing is, I think, the most productive. These are the slender-bodied, sparsely-dressed flies beloved of generations of North Country anglers—delicate, unbulky little things, with a few wisps of straggly hackle which imitate the nymph's straggly bits of antennae and legs quite cunningly. I am very partial to the thin North and West Country spiders: they catch fish.

The other sort of old-fashioned wet fly, that is tied with a wing set close in to the body, is not to be despised completely, for the slender hump of wing does more or less represent the wing-case of the nymph. However, it is not (I think) in the same class as the spider or the true-tied imitative nymph, and I use it hardly at all. There is one exception to this rule of mine, the March Brown; but of that, more later.

Now for fishing it. Upstream wet-fly fishing is the most upstream of all types of fly fishing. The dry-fly fisherman will tell you that he fishes upstream, but, in fact, he more often fishes obliquely or even directly across the stream. The upstream wet-fly man or nymph fisher fishes *almost* directly upstream. He has to.

Consider what we have to attempt. We have to pitch a nymph into the water so that it has time to sink a bit and then come drifting downstream with the current, exactly at the rate of the current, rising and falling a little. You cannot manage that unless you cast almost directly upstream.

It follows that upstream wet-fly or nymph fishing is most easily and efficiently managed when you are standing in the water. For although you can cast up under your own bank *from* the bank, you cannot search the middle of the stream, or the far bank, unless you are more or less in line with them. This is one case when wading is almost a necessity, and certainly an advantage. On a river of any size, that is. You can search the whole of a small river from one bank, of course.

But the wader certainly scores on a river of some breadth. And you *must* learn to wade properly, otherwise you are going to ruin your own fishing and everybody else's within hundreds of yards. Enter the water as slowly and quietly as possible. Don't tramp through it, throwing up a bow-wave and stirring up mud. Never move a foot without care. Take your time.

Move as if you were sneaking into a sleeping house. And you will find, if you do it carefully enough, that fish will swim around your wadered legs without suspicion. But one careless, hasty move, and you will see them shooting away upstream, communicating their alarm to every fish within hundreds of yards.

The late Lord Glanusk, one of the finest upstream wet-fly fishers in the country, used to catch *a majority* of his fish within four yards of his legs. Let that be your target. (I believe that he caught most of them on a March Brown nymph.)

And you will have made another deduction from all this—namely, that long casting is not necessary in this game. Quite right. Long casting is neither necessary nor desirable. Short casts and crafty wading are two of the most important things. The third—and most difficult—is hooking the fish.

There are two distinct styles of upstream wet-fly fishing, one respectably ancient, the other fairly modern. I wouldn't like to say which is the more productive.

The old style is to fish a team of wet flies—preferably spiders—well sunk, on an ungreased cast and, more often than not, an ungreased line. This style is often used when you are methodically searching the whole of the water.

The second style is to fish just one nymph on a cast which is greased down to within a foot or so of the fly. The line, too, is greased, as in dry-fly fishing. The fly (nymph) is cast as a dry fly is cast, to a rising fish or to a spot where it is expected that an unseen fish may be lying. In fact, the only difference between this style of nymphing and plain dry-fly fishing is that the fly is sunk a little way—only a few inches—below the surface.

Obviously, your choice of method depends greatly on the nature of the water which you are fishing. If you are fishing 'chalk-stream style' water, you are more likely to cast to fish which you have actually spotted, as the pukka chalk-stream dry-fly man does. In that case you will use one nymph, greased line, and semi-greased cast. But if you are fishing more or less at random on a fairly dark, fairly turbulent water—almost anywhere, that is to say, in the North and West—you will not have the same opportunities of spotting a given individual fish and stalking him. Therefore, on such a river—and such rivers very greatly outnumber the crystal clear, placid chalk streams—it will pay you to fish a team of wet flies on an ungreased cast and (often) an ungreased line.

Even though you are fishing in this second method, do not think that the good man merely flogs away aimlessly, putting his flies down anywhere on the water. You slowly develop a sense of watermanship. You come to read the surface of the broken water—and from the surface you deduce the bottom. There is always a measure of detective work in fly fishing.

In the section on fly fishing for coarse fish I give you some hints on where to look for the fish, but here we are thinking generally of trout fishing. Now trout in broken water—in all moorland and mountain streams, in practically all the wild and rushing rivers of the North and West—take what shelter they can find. This shelter is almost always provided by the geography of the river-bed.

Where there is a boulder, the current will have scoured out a depression all round it. Trout may be lying immediately upstream and immediately downstream of the boulder, and they may also, though less often, be lying right in at the sides of it. In these lays they escape the full force of the current, but they are in a good position to nip out and snatch any morsels of food that may go drifting past.

Equally, a depression in the river-bed will provide a lie for a fish, for the current rushing straight downstream leaves a pocket of calmer water in the depression.

So all such places may hold fish. You learn to interpret swirls and boils on the surface, even when you cannot actually see the rocks which cause them. And you fish your flies, not in the smooth, unbroken water, but wherever a swirl or turbulence suggests a hidden rock. And, of course, you carefully fish all around rocks which you *can* see.

Lastly, I should hardly need to say, if you actually see fish rising, you fish for them.

I don't want to give the impression that smooth glides are never productive. Frequently they *are*, but it all depends on the degree of cover available to the fish. Trout especially, but all fish to some extent, like to remain near their own particular 'homes'—lies where they can rest out of the worst of the current and where they also feel relatively secure and inconspicuous. (For fish have their enemies in the water, of course, ranging from otters to other predatory fish.)

One typical instance of smooth water well worth fishing is the deep side of a bend. On every bend the current, trying to flow straight on, has hollowed out a deep bay on the inside of the bend, which shallows off towards the other bank. The deep inside piece of water, though often tranquil as to surface and not so obviously fishy, will usually hold a fish or two.

Other places well worth searching with your flies are holes beneath overhanging trees—the harder to reach, the more likely to be the holt of a good fish—and the white water right under a waterfall. It may look so rapid and fierce that no fish could possibly hold a place in it; but there is a sort of 'vacuum' under the pelmet of white water where things are relatively calm —a 'vertical eddy', in fact—and here there is often a fish or two, for a waterfall brings down a lot of food. On a stifling hot day, such is probably the best cast of all.

Just above a fall, too, almost on the very brink, you may find a fish, and at the sides of fierce, fast currents fish like to lie in the relatively slow water, ready to dash into the current to snatch a morsel floating by.

The mechanics of fishing the upstream wet fly are

not too easy to master, but they are simple enough, in essence, and well worth the slight effort. Let me admit here and now that this is the most difficult of all forms of fly fishing, bar none. To the expert, perhaps the most productive.

Let us get the worst over first—the fishing of a team of wet flies on an ungreased leader. The line may or may not float—it depends on the depth of the water you are fishing. As a general rule, I think, we may say that it will help if the line floats down to about six feet from its end. That leaves you with two yards of un-greased line and an ungreased leader. Since your leader will probably be three yards long, it means, theoretic-ally, that you can search water five yards deep. But that would be true only if your ungreased line and leader were dangling down vertically into the water. In prac-tice, your flies—which are always being swept towards you by the current, remember—will get down about a couple of feet at the most, and rather more likely a couple of inches. It all depends on the distance you throw and the speed of the current. The longer they have to travel, the deeper they will sink. The milder the current, the deeper they will sink. In practice, with the very short casts you make in this business, your flies will rarely get down more than a yard, I should say. But it is almost impossible to generalise. Anyway, a yard is enough, as a rule. Feeding fish will not be hug-ging the bed of the stream. And some of the streams which you will be fishing will not be much more than a yard deep.

This form of upstream wet-fly fishing is the busiest and most active of all aspects of fly fishing. Using the downstream method as described in the previous chap-ter, you make one cast and let it fish itself out, which takes quite a time, and then you move a few yards and start again. Fishing the dry fly, as you will see later, you make a cast and then have an appreciable 'waiting period' while the fly completes its drift on the surface. (Moreover, if you cast only to rising fish you may have hours of idleness.) But when fishing the wet-fly team upstream you are working all the time. Obviously, the moment your flies pitch into the water they start coming back to you.

In fact, I would go so far as to say that the flies are not in the water for more than two or three yards—and it doesn't take very long for them to travel that far. So you are casting all the time.

You will now see the logic behind the short cast which is recommended. (And the light, easy-on-the-wrist rod.) It is very easy to chuck the flies many yards upstream—but how are you to keep in touch with them as they drift back to you? It can't be done. You can raise the rod tip and you can strip line in desperately with the left hand—but you will still be left with an uncontrolled and uncontrollable bunch of line piling up between you and your flies.

The answer is the very short cast. And the very long rod some would add, but I don't go quite so far as that myself. The best technique, I think, is to make a short cast almost directly upstream. The moment your flies sink, start to tighten up the line by raising the rod tip and by drawing in line with your left hand. Even so, you can only keep in touch with your flies during a drift of about two or three yards at most. Then you have to remove them from the water and cast again. It's thirsty work.

You will have deduced that for this exercise a light rod, not too whippy, is ideal. True. It should not be too stiff either, for you are casting a very short line indeed, and a stiff rod will not begin to do any work itself until you have a fair weight of line out beyond the rod top. On the other hand, if it is *too* soft you may find it tricky to hook your fish, for the strike has to be instantaneous in this style of fishing. I like a nine-foot rod for this, as for most forms of fly fishing, and it should be definitely a lightweight—a heavy rod will take a lot of the fun out of fishing.

This is definitely one occasion when the cheap level

line comes into its own. With a double-tapered line, the heavy part comes into action only when you have a fair length of line out. A level line starts to work the rod much sooner, and since you are never concerned to 'shoot' line in this exercise, the level line's reluctance to shoot through the rod rings doesn't matter at all. A forward-taper or torpedo-head line is pleasant to use, but a level line at a third the price is perfect for the job.

So there it is. Cast. Raise the rod top and draw in line with the left hand. Lift and cast again. Move forward quietly all the time, searching new water and likely spots. Don't stand and flog away at the same piece of water. If you didn't raise 'em the first time, you probably won't raise 'em at all.

But how to tell when a fish has mouthed one of your flies? Ah, that is exactly the crux of the whole business. The great upstream wet-fly fisher develops a new instinct, a sixth sense. Sometimes you get some help. Sometimes you see 'the little golden wink under water' as a fish turns with your fly. Sometimes you notice that the drift downstream has been checked. Sometimes the line moves slightly sideways as it comes down towards you. All these are pointers, and if any of these things happens—or if you only *think* it is happening—strike smartly.

But there are innumerable occasions when the good wet-fly man hooks a fish and then, under pressure, cannot honestly tell you why he struck. It *is* something that looks very like an 'instinct'; it comes only of experience. You fish for years and you begin to know how your line behaves as it comes back to you, and you find yourself detecting the slightest variation from its normal behaviour and reacting to that variation by striking. Any good man will confirm what I am telling you.

It may make you feel that this is too difficult, but believe me, it is tremendously well worthwhile to persevere. In this method, your flies drift downstream so naturally, more naturally than in any other method: not surprisingly, they deceive fish more readily than flies fished any other way. If only you can develop that instinct that tells you when to raise the rod tip sharply, you will find yourself catching many more fish than by any other method you care to name.

Some wet-fly men give their flies a certain movement under water by waggling the rod slightly, to make the nymphs rise and fall. It works, no doubt, but it can be overdone, and anyway while you are a learner at this game you will find yourself fully occupied in keeping the line reasonably straight from rod tip to flies. The water itself, of course, acting on the hackles, gives the flies a certain air of natural life. No current is absolutely even and uniform: anything drifting down in it has a certain motion, apart from its general downstream motion. So don't worry about waggling the rod tip—not, at any rate, until you have mastered the art of keeping a true touch with your flies. It is amazing how a really good man *feels* the flies on the end of his line. They become a projection of himself, he is aware of what is happening to them although he cannot see them.

There it is, then, in outline: the most tricky, the most active, and perhaps the most rewarding method of fishing a fly. I can only recommend any novice to persevere. I had to myself. And I have come to love it.

*   *   *   *   *

The second method of upstream wet-fly fishing, as I said, is true nymph fishing, closely akin to dry-fly fishing. In this practice you grease the line, and you may even grease the leader, except for the last foot or two.

You pitch your nymph in the water upstream and let it drift down past a likely lay, or where you have seen a fish rising, or wherever you have seen a bulge on the water made by a fish taking nymphs underneath the surface.

Since the nymph fishes so close to the surface, you have a fair chance of seeing any rise to it—there will either be a disturbance on the surface, a swirl or 'hump', or you will actually see the flash of the fish. Alternatively, if you see nothing of the fish, you will notice that your leader draws underwater slightly, or just stops drifting downstream. Or, if you are watching the knot where your leader joins your line, you will see it pull and/or skid. Or, again, there will be a slight sideways skid of the leader where it disappears into the water.

All these signs mean that a fish has taken the nymph into its mouth. All demand an instantaneous strike. You cannot be too quick, for when you spot the sign the fish is already on the point of ejecting this crude deception which it has taken into its mouth. And until you have actually seen it happen you won't believe how fast and powerfully a fish can eject something which it finds suspect and disappointing.

Nymph fishing is highly productive, and very much easier than genuine old-style upstream wet-fly fishing with a sunken team. You need not concentrate so closely on casting almost directly upstream. You can cast obliquely upstream across the current, as one often has to cast a dry fly. When the intermediate current between you and your nymph causes the line to belly and the nymph to drag, its erratic action across the current will not necessarily put a wary fish off, as it would if you were fishing the floating fly.

A nymph, after all, has *some* independent life of its own; it is not merely sitting inertly on the surface being carried downstream by a current over which it has no power whatsoever. A nymph *might* make a bit of a kick and do a sort of sideways swim across an under-surface current—and a fish would not necessarily be put off by this, since a fish knows a nymph to be a swimming and struggling thing with intentions of its own. So the cross-current cast is not necessarily wasted because drag brings the nymph swerving across the current. Indeed, the first moment of such drag often helps a fish to make up its mind, and brings it chasing determinedly after a nymph which it might not have bothered to take on an inert drift.

Even so, it is normally good practice to pitch the nymph in pretty well upstream and let it come down unhindered. You draw in line with the left hand just as you do in upstream wet-fly fishing with a team—but in this case, since your line is floating, you don't have to work quite so hard and fast at it.

In clear chalk streams nymph fishing is not only productive but also exquisitely fascinating. You can sometimes see the whole thing—see the fish rise to the nymph (even though you can't see the nymph itself, of course)—see the mouth open whitely as the fish takes the nymph, and see the jaws close as the fish sinks down again. This is marvellous fun, but it doesn't happen very often, to most anglers, who have to take their fishing on rather murkier, rougher waters than the exquisite chalk streams of the balmy south.

The best rod for nymph fishing is your dry-fly rod. It has to pitch the nymph with great accuracy when you are fishing for an individual fish, already spotted. It has to be very smart on the strike. Whatever rod you have chosen for dry-fly fishing is the right rod for nymph fishing too.

Indeed, for all upstream fishing one rod will do. And it should not be too short—a longish rod, nine feet at any rate, is a great help in managing that downstream drift.

That has dealt, then, with old-style downstream wet-fly fishing, with old-style upstream wet-fly fishing, with true nymph fishing in the modern manner. Now I will give you a résumé of orthodox dry-fly fishing—and, after that, I will put you on to my own favourite method, which is neither wet nor dry, but both.

And which I believe to be exceptionally effective.

Not because I invented it, for I didn't.

CHAPTER 12

The Orthodox Dry Fly

Dry-fly fishing is often spoken of with a touch of awe, as if it were the holiest-of-holies in angling, the absolute peak and summit of skill and knowledge. Confirmed dry-fly purists are not averse to spreading this view.

In fact, to be blunt, dry-fly fishing, though quite delightful, is by far the easiest method of taking fish. It is easier than fishing a worm, far easier than fishing a wet fly upstream, even easier than intelligent spinning. In dry fly fishing you see the fish take your fly and your hooking problem is solved for you.

So absurd is the edifice of snobbery which has grown up around dry-fly fishing that it is almost impossible, at this stage, to disentangle the separate strands of idiocy. Not so very long ago *all* fly fishing, even on the Test, was wet-fly fishing—downstream, the old easy style. Then somebody invented dry-fly fishing—*to make it easier to catch fish*. It was taken up by all the powers of snobbish propaganda, which are enormous, and by the end of the nineteenth century it was on a pinnacle of holiness. Dry-fly purists actually argue, these days, that dry-fly fishing is *more* difficult: that they fish the dry-fly in order to preserve stocks, which would be indiscriminately slaughtered by wet-fly fishing. Rubbish, in short. On a well-stocked chalk stream —and that was the home of dry fly—it is easier to catch fish with the floater than with the sunk fly, for the water is so clear that the man who fishes downstream reveals himself and his gear far too much. Wherever fish rise freely and there is plenty of fly life, as in the chalk streams, it is easier to pick them off with the floating fly. So it is absurd for dry-fly purists to give themselves airs—not only for knowledge but also for sportsmanship.

On dusky, turbulent rivers, on the other hand, the dry fly is less effective. Unless there is a good hatch to bring fish on the rise to surface food, sunk fly will kill more fish.

Now dry-fly fishing consists of putting down on the surface of the water, very lightly, an imitation of a dun which has just hatched, or a spent fly (or spinner) which has returned to the water to lay its eggs, and to die. You pitch the fly on to the water just upstream of where you have seen a fish rise, and let it ride down. If you have done it about right, the fish gulps in the fly, you actually see it happen; as the fish turns down again, you tighten up and the fish is hooked. What could be simpler?

Assuming that fish are actually rising to hatching fly, you have only two problems. First, to put up an acceptable imitation of—*or alternative to*—the natural hatching insect. Second, to place it almost on the fish's nose without scaring the fish.

In Chapter 15 I deal briefly with identification of the natural insect and choice of the correct artificial. But to be bluntly honest, this isn't really so very important—at least, not so important as dyed-in-the-wool chalk-stream men aver. The trouble is that a disproportionately large percentage of fly-fishing literature has been written by chalk-stream men. For them, admittedly, it *is* very important to choose the right artificial: fat chalk-stream trout *do* grow fussy about their diet, and *do* often refuse all but one particular species of fly. But for most of us, fishing less well-favoured (and less expensive) waters, the choice of the right fly is a good deal less important than you would think if you read only the scholarly works of the chalk-stream entomologists. Thank goodness.

Mark you, I am not sneering at the chalk-stream chaps. Not at all. They have the luck to fish marvellous well-stocked waters, and they *do* have to solve the peculiar problems of those waters, where trout see clearly a long way through gin-clear water and grow fussy about their food. For most of us, trout fishing means fishing in waters where the trout can't see so far and are nowhere near so well fed; consequently, they are a good deal less fussy. I don't begrudge the chalk-stream chaps their fun: they have made a delightful bit of whimsy out of their private culture of angling entomology. But it has much less relevance to our own probable angling.

On the ordinary waters which you and I are more likely to fish, trout are usually too hungry to be over-choosy. True, your fly must pass muster *as a fly*: it must appear natural, and it must behave naturally. The two basic rules operate without exception. But a hungry trout, on the feed, will, I verily believe, take almost any fly that measures up to those basic desiderata.

Chalk-stream experts go in for the most minute particularity as to shade of hackle, number of whisks, type of wing, and so on. Perhaps they have to, perhaps it is all just a glorious game. Certainly they do, often, have to go to great pains to get a fly which the fish wants *now*. We humbler mortals, fishing the less costly waters, need not be quite so fastidious. Be sure our trout will not! I would go so far as to say that if we choose a fly that is about the right size, well tied, as translucent as may be, and one that sits nicely up on the water—then, if we present it properly, the trout will take it without hesitation whatever its colour may be. Better men than I have proved this by determined trial.

I will go farther. I will affirm that one pattern of fly—one chosen almost at random out of the thousands and thousands of patterns available—will take fish throughout the season, provided that you have it available in a range of sizes and that you fish it well.

True, you are sure to hit the day when the fish are 'mad on' one particular fly and will not look at anything else. I agree. It *does* happen, and not only on chalk streams. But it happens so rarely, on the majority of waters available to the average, fairly impecunious angler, that you can take a chance on it. By and large, you can take a steady toll of trout with just one of the following general patterns—provided, as I say, that you have it available in several different sizes, from very small to very large, and that you fish it intelligently:

Greenwell's Glory   Wickham's Fancy
Pheasant Tail   Gold-ribbed Hare's Ear
Coch-y-Bonddhu   Dry Bloody Butcher
Black Spider   Red Spinner
Iron Blue Dun   Blue Upright

That list of ten flies contains ten deadly killers. Not one of them is a hit-and-miss fly. On their day all will lure fish. And there are many more—thousands more. I have given you a short list of flies in which you may have great confidence. I will add one more, a tremendous stand-by which has done great execution:

Tup's Indispensable

I would not, myself, very much like to be confined to a Tup, and no other, and therefore I do not include it in the list of flies to almost any one of which I would not mind being strictly confined. But it is a very great fly on its day—a bright day, for preference.

That dry Bloody Butcher will surprise any expert who might be wasting his time reading this elementary treatise. But I have found it a terrific little number. Tied with a plain body of gold tinsel, and hackled fairly heavily in a mixture of red and black, it looks like nothing that ever flew. I can only say that, although it represents nothing in creation, it takes trout with conspicuous and consistent success. For me, at any rate.

That's an important point. A fly is only as good as its fisherman. It isn't the slightest use fishing a fly which you don't like. You must have confidence in your fly. Why this is so, I have no idea. But every experienced angler knows it to be true. It would be too far-fetched to suggest that somehow your confidence is transmitted to your artificial fly. But that is what *seems* to happen.

When you are fishing a fly which you like, you fish it with confidence, and that means that you do everything meticulously, believing that you have a real chance of interesting a fish if you do your own part properly. Whereas if you tie on a fly in which you have no confidence, you find yourself fishing listlessly, carelessly, casually. And, oddly enough, this means that you catch nothing. It has been proved over and over again. Many a team of friendly anglers has proved it.

One man has great faith in, say, Greenwell's Glory. Another has not, but he has faith in the Medium Olive Dun (which is as like the Greenwell as makes no odds, for they both represent the same thing). Each will take fish, fishing his favourite fly. But if they swap flies, *neither* will touch a fish. It's fantastic, but it's true.

Me, now, I cannot fish Greenwell's Glory at all. (Though I include it in my list.) For me, it has no magic. Yet I doubt if there has ever been tied a fly which has enjoyed such consistent success. Canon Greenwell, may he rest in peace, is commemorated by a fly that would more or less represent all the Olives, light, medium, dark, lake, and rough. His is a very great fly indeed. Why it won't fish for me, I have no idea. I can only say that I have never caught a trout on it. Not one. That must be very nearly a unique experience among trout fishermen. I include it in my short list, all the same, because it is a universal favourite, a proven all-rounder.

Yet I confidently fish that monstrosity the dry Butcher. And catch fish with it. You see how much faith has to do with it.

Now please don't think that I am denigrating the game of matching the insect on the water. By no means. Angling entomology is a fascinating sideline to fishing, absorbing if you happen to like it, boring if you have no inclination that way. Any man's particular study is to be respected: angling entomologists have contributed a great deal to angling literature, if, perhaps, rather less to angling. It is a very pleasant game if it appeals to you. All I am trying to do is to make it clear to the novice that there is no need to be intimidated by the complexity of the literature on this subject of fly fishing.

It is not easy, but it isn't at all difficult. If you can catch roach consistently in clearish water, you can catch trout with the fly, equally consistently. If it happens to appeal to you, that is—and presumably it does, or you would not be reading this book. Some steady float fishers find that they have no sympathy with fly fishing. They never take to it because they are temperamentally unsuited to it. They are static fishers. Very well. But anyone who is interested in and attracted by the active, graceful, and fluent practice of fly fishing can become a fairly effective dry-fly angler within a season. That is my sole object: to tear away some of the clouds of hokum that surround the subject, to encourage you to believe that you, too, can become a good dry-fly angler without the need to know, or care, *very* much about the entomology of the river.

Naturally, it adds to your proficiency, and probably to your interest, to be able to identify the different flies. But not one fly fisherman in a thousand *can*. Don't be discouraged if they all look alike to you. *Take local advice on flies*. That is a golden rule, and so obvious that I should be ashamed to print it did I not know that thousands of anglers never think of doing so. Take local advice, wherever you may be. You won't be the first man to fish that water! Use the local flies first. If you make no headway with them, then start experimenting on your own.

However, of flies and imitations I treat in Chapter 15. Now for the mechanics of the job.

*   *   *   *   *

The mechanical technique of dry-fly fishing falls into two branches: fishing the rise, and fishing the water. The first means simply, waiting and watching until you see a fish rise to the surface and suck in a fly. Thereafter you offer him a fly which you think he might take—preferably, some would say certainly, an imitation of the fly which you just saw him take. The second means putting your fly down on the water in all spots where you think a fish may be lurking on the look-out for food, even if you don't see a sign of a fin.

The first is pukka. The second is sensible.

The first is so easy that almost no more need be said about it. The second is active, interesting, and can add up to hard work. It can also save you from total boredom on a day when fish are not rising.

The great enemy of the dry-fly fisherman is *drag*. Let me explain drag.

Say you see a fish rise. He is lying on the far side of the river. (He would be.) He lies in fairly smooth water, not travelling very fast. You can reach him easily. But between you and the fish there is a fast run. You make a neat cast and drop your fly beautifully a yard ahead of the ring made by the rising fish. Theoretically you should catch him.

But your line has fallen across the faster current that runs between you and your fish. This current immediately begins to pull the line downstream at a great rate. The fly, though, and part of the leader, or all of it, has fallen in quieter water beyond the fast run. So what happens?

Obviously, the belly-body of the line, being carried downstream by the current, pulls the fly along with it. If all the surface of the stream were travelling at the same rate the fly would float down undisturbed at the

rate of the stream. But it is being pulled—dragged—
by that part of the line which is being carried downstream by the faster current. Therefore the fly skates
across the surface of the quieter water. It is dragged. It
scars the surface. It makes a thoroughly unnatural V
wake. It behaves as no fly ever behaves, travelling
faster than the current which bears it. Your fish
observes this and leaves it severely alone. Wouldn't
you?

That, then, is drag, the dry-fly man's bugbear. And,
such is the peremptory cussedness of life, you will
usually find *good* trout lying where they are protected
from the wiles of the dry-fly angler by just such a
combination of varying current speeds. That is why
they have grown up to be good trout. The better the
fish, the more likely he is to have taken up a position
where he can get at food without much effort, but
where he is protected from the fly fisherman either by
a thicket of overhanging branches, weeds, et cetera, or
where he is protected by a combination of water speeds
—surface speeds, at any rate—which might have been
especially designed to give him full warning of the
phoneyness of the fly fisher's fly. I don't suppose the fish
actually has enough brains to have reasoned it all out,
but at any rate, that is what he does. Whether it be
'instinct' or 'reason', the result is just the same for the
angler: frustration.

What do you do about that? Luckily, there are
several things you may do.

Basically, you have so to organise your throw that
the fly remains undisturbed long enough to deceive
your fish. The first thing you do is to throw your fly as
near to the fish as possible without actually hitting
him on the nose. Reduce the period of float to a minimum. Place it a mere foot above the fish, at most.

That is the first part of the job, and perhaps the
easiest. Anyone who can cast at all well can place a fly
on a saucer four times out of five. It is purely and
simply a matter of practice. You won't be able to do it

without a lot of practice. Put a saucer on the lawn and cast at it—or, I should say, *over* it—for hours on end. Never mind what the neighbours think. Accuracy you must have, if you are to become a good dry-fly man.

The second part of the job is to throw either a curved or a crooked line. The idea is that it will take the fast part of the current a few moments to pull this crooked part of the line straight, and while the line is straightening the fly floats on undisturbed, perfectly natural-looking. Whereas if your line falls on the water perfectly straight, drag sets in immediately.

You might think that it is the easiest thing in the world to throw a crooked line. It is, really, but unfortunately you have spent a lot of time (I hope) practising to throw a *straight* line. For wet-fly fishing you *must* be able to throw a straight line. Well, now you must unlearn that excellent technique.

To get a wavy crookedness into your line is very easy. You get out just as much line as is needed to put the fly down exactly where you want it (by false casting, of course, without letting the line fall on to the water). Then you pull another yard or two off the reel, while still false casting. Now, if you released this extra line gently and smoothly at the right moment on the forward cast, your line would go out perfectly straight, and your fly would fall a yard or two too far out, beyond your fish.

But you don't release it smoothly. You release it with a bang, putting lots of snap and power into your forward cast—which is aimed, I repeat, not at the water but a yard *above* the water, into thin air. The result is that your line goes whistling out like an express train, streams out to its full limit, *and bounces back*. It is this bounce back which matters. Instead of lowering your rod point and finishing out the cast in the proper way, you check the rod on the forward stroke. You will *feel* the snatch at the rod top as the line reaches the limit of its travel and is brutally pulled back. (You can achieve the same effect without shooting line, merely by casting too far and pulling your rod back as the fly is about to fall.)

Result—your line falls untidily on the water in a series of curves. It looks very ugly. But if you have judged it right your fly has fallen in the right place, and there it floats serenely for a second or two, while the fast current between you and your fish is busy straightening out the crookedness of the line.

(If, when you are first learning to cast, you find that this *always* happens—when you don't want it to, when you are aiming to aspiring to get out a nice straight line—then it means that you are putting far too much energy into your forward cast. Relax.)

The deliberate crooked line is the standard way of beating drag. It isn't the only way, but it is perhaps the very easiest. The other way is to throw a deliberate bend—the famous 'shepherd's crook'. Since this is beyond me, except occasionally and by accident, I should be very wrong to lay down the law on how to do it. I find that if I make a *horizontal* cast, with the rod travelling pretty well parallel with the water, under my own bank, I can usually manage to do a nice shepherd's crook turning to the right. I do this by checking the cast just when the rod line is straightening out. But I haven't yet been able to make a left-handed curve to order. Perhaps a left-hand angler would find it as easy as I, a right-hander, find the right-handed curve. I expect he would. You must try, for it is undoubtedly a most useful cast. The curve gives the fly time to ride nicely for a few moments before the intervening current starts to pull or drag it. And another thing: by casting a nice curve, you present the fly to the fish without giving him a chance of seeing much gut, if any. This is most important. See what you can do. Everyone casts slightly differently.

Anyway, the curve is a very useful throw when you are casting almost straight upstream, but the crooked line will serve you very well when you are casting almost directly across the stream. And this is how the majority of so-called 'upstream' fly fishing is done, I think—and why not? The less chance there is of the fish seeing your gut, the better your chance of deluding him into taking your fly.

Another way of defeating drag, when you are fishing to a riser under the far bank, is to go upstream of him and cast downstream and across. This gives him a look at your fly before he sees your gut, and, obviously, it gives the fly a moment to float properly before the line catches up with it.

Many a time, when faced with a fish rising within inches of the far bank, and a strong current running in between me and him, I have adopted a little stratagem which either pays off handsomely or breaks your heart. This is to cast a shade too far, so that your fly becomes lodged in the vegetation of the far bank, slightly upstream of the fish—only inches upstream. You then twitch your line gently, and either find that your fly is inextricably embedded in the vegetation, which causes bad thoughts, or it drops right on to the fish's nose and he takes it without a moment's hesitation. It is a good trick, for fish that lie close in under the bank *do* find a fair number of living things dropping in from the overhanging vegetation, and accept them without question. You make the cast, of course, standing well upstream of the fish, so that no drag occurs when the fly falls—it is well in advance of the line.

To do this takes a certain nerve, or recklessness. It all depends on how much you want the fish, how much you want the fly. To me, any fish is worth a fly. Anglers are divided into those who put an unduly high value on their tackle and those who think a fish is worth a lure. The first sort catch fewer fish than they would catch if they adventured their flies into the difficult-looking spots—under overhanging branches, for example. The second sort lose a lot of flies and leaders, but they rise a great many fine fish, and even land some of them. Spinners are bigger sinners than fly fishers in this respect: spinning lures cost so much that spinners are naturally reluctant to fish them over bad bottoms deeply and slowly. But you can say as an axiom that the best fish are *always* in the most difficult places.

You may have noticed that although dry-fly fishing is usually thought of as being always 'upstream' fishing —in order to remain unseen by the fish, which lie with their heads upstream of their tails—I personally don't mind getting above the fish and casting downstream. I would go so far as to say that there are times when you can only hope to catch certain difficult fish by fishing downstream to them. This is often true of those tricky beasts which take up a secure lie under overhanging trees on your own side of the river. If you are standing on the true left bank of the river, you may be able to cast a right-hand bend which shows the fly to the fish before he sees the gut. I can sometimes manage this. But if you are standing on the true right bank, you may find it as difficult as I do to throw a left-handed curve. The answer, or at least *one* answer, is to move a few yards upstream of the fish and send the fly down to him.

There are two ways of doing this. If the geography of the place permits, you may simply drop your fly on the water and walk down with it—a sort of mobile dapping. I have done it many a time, and it can succeed. I wouldn't pretend that it is fly fishing as she is understood. The other way is to cast a 'bouncer'— cast a line that bounces back when you check the rod, so that the line falls on the water in a snakey wriggle, and the fly travels on ahead calmly and serenely until all the line has straightened out. When doing this trick you aim directly downstream, of course. Either it comes off first time or it fails—you have only one chance.

If you have gauged correctly the amount of line to throw, it can be brilliantly successful. The fly floats down ahead of the gut and line, unworried by drag, exactly at the pace of the current, and it is fair odds that the fish will take it. Of course, if he doesn't, eventually your line is lying straight downstream and can travel no farther, the fly begins to kick up a fuss on the surface, held as it is against the current. To get it back without making more fuss is virtually impossible, and your fish has been put well and truly down. However, since there's no other way, it's always well worth trying.

Dry fly used to be thought suitable only for placid, smooth-surfaced glides: another legacy of the chalk-stream man's moral ascendancy. Fairly recently it has been found to be quite effective on fast water, and the modern silicone fly floatants make it easy to keep the fly perfectly buoyant even on a racing stream. Never fail to search the edges of fast tear-away currents—trout may not lie right in the fast water, but they often lie at the very edge of a fast current—and there is often calm water beneath a fast top layer. There is nothing nicer than to see a cocky little fly riding buoyantly down a bobbing current—except, of course, to see it suddenly vanish, engulfed by a fish's neb. This is a very effective way of fishing shallow, fast streams bobbling over broken ground, especially shallow water. Of course, the fly comes back to you so fast that it is quite hard work, almost as hard as upstream wet-fly fishing. You are casting all the time. But it is very jolly, and often quite productive.

I must say just another word about the modern silicone fly floatants. They have made a world of difference to the game. In the old way, you anointed your fly with oil or with a line grease. Either way, it left rings of oil on the surface—a very bad thing—and it floated indifferently well. Hence the incessant false casting to dry the fly between drifts—very hard work, very tough on rod and wrist. The new silicones are marvellous: they waterproof the fly for long periods.

The spread of silicone floatants, coupled with un-sinkable lines, has affected the design of rods. The terrific power of a conventional dry-fly rod—the stiffness which makes it such a tiring and unpleasant thing to use—was largely necessitated by this incessant switching back and fro in the air, which puts a great strain on the butt especially. When your fly is an automatic floater, you can cut out the false casting to a great degree, if not entirely. This means that your rod can be not only lighter but also more limber and gentle. At any rate, I now use almost nothing but a wet-fly rod, so-called, for all purposes. Unless there is a gale blowing, in which case you do more or less have to resort to a stiffer, tougher rod in order to throw a much heavier line. But with me, at any rate, this is a last resort.

Because I don't really despise the chalk-stream man's fascinated absorption in entomology, I give a chapter on fly identification and imitation. If you are going to fish chalk or chalk-style streams, you certainly must learn it up, *and* read the recommended books on the subject, *and* learn all you can from the *habitués* of the water. But apart from that, there is nothing more which I have to say about orthodox dry-fly fishing. Let's pass on to the method which is neither dry nor wet, but more effective than either.

CHAPTER 13

Neither Dry nor Wet

I just don't know why this method is not practised
more widely. It combines the advantages of both dry-
and wet-fly fishing, and avoids at any rate *some* of the
drawbacks of both.

It is very simple. A countryman who never reads a
book first showed it to me. Since I took it up I have
read about it, not often but occasionally, in writings
by obviously wily and successful fish-catchers. Nowadays I always use it, unless it happens to be prohibited on the particular water which I am fishing, or
unless special circumstances dictate that one or other
of the conventional methods will beat it on the day.

Pre-eminently it is a method for strange waters and
'off' days, when nothing particular is doing.

That is to say, it is a method for the majority of
days.

You arrive at a strange river-side. You put up your
rod, bursting with hope. You thread the line through
the rods rings and attach a leader. Then you start looking at the water, hoping for some sign of busy, feeding
fish.

Not a sign. Not a swirl, not a wrinkle on the water's
skin to guide you. You have to fish blind, using all the
accumulated water-craft and instinct for fishy places
that you have laboriously acquired.

And 'the method'.

It is an exceedingly simple method. You simply tie
on both a dry fly *and* a nymph, and methodically
search all the likely places with them.

Thus equipped, and using the equipment reasonably, you stand a better than fair chance of attracting
any fish that is at all interested in feeding.

There are two schools of thought about where you tie which fly. For a long time I tied the nymph on the extreme point of the leader, and the dry fly on a short dropper about one to two feet away from the nymph. But fairly recently I have tried switching them, using the dry fly on the point just like an orthodox dry-fly angler, and the nymph on a rather longer-than-usual dropper some two feet away from the point. I am inclined to favour this second method, for then the dry fly, riding up and down merrily on a brisk current, lifts the nymph up and down as it rises and falls. This must give a very life-like motion to the nymph. It is true that this will happen to some extent whichever tying you use, but with the dry fly at the point and the nymph on a short dropper nearer the rod, I guess that the dry fly exerts a more direct influence on the up-and-down movement of the nymph. I incline to favour it, too, because it casts rather better—if the nymph on its dropper twists round the main leader it matters rather less than if the dry fly twists round it. Moreover, the nymph hanging straight down into the water makes the 'network' of gut at the junction less conspicuous.

I expect that you will have perceived already the very particular advantage of this method. It is not simply that you are giving the fish a choice between dry fly and wet—though that is often an advantage well worth taking. No, the chief beauty of this method is that the dry fly acts precisely as a float, and gives the most apathetic or inattentive angler ample warning when a fish takes his underwater fly.

I told you, earlier, that upstream wet-fly fishing was real hard work and that it demanded a sort of instinct for when to strike. This method cuts out the uncertainty to a very great extent. When a fish mouths your nymph you will almost certainly be aware of it—your dry fly may actually be pulled under water, more probably it will skid or skate sideways, or stop dead, or in some other plain and unmistakable way tell you

that a fish has hold of your nymph. You lift smartly
and hook him.

That is really all there is to it.

It makes upstream wet-fly fishing as easy as upstream
dry-fly fishing—but much more productive.

I ought to tell you that traditional upstream wet-fly
men often use the topmost of three flies as a sort of
indicator, if not precisely as a float. If you use a team
of three flies and your top fly (nearest the rod) is a
fairly bushy, well-hackled specimen, it will probably
never get truly sunk, but will remain awash. So long as
you can see it, it will act as an indicator for you. However, it is not so clear-cut as this method of one true
floater and one sunk nymph.

You fish your flies, of course, just as you would fish
the dry fly or the nymph. That is to say, you search all
the likely spots, mainly casting more or less upstream
at a more or less oblique angle, depending on how
accessible the fishy spot is. It is a marvellous method
for the careful wader, casting a short line ahead of him
as he eases his way slowly, so slowly, up-river.

A characteristic team of two, with which to start the
day when you have no idea what flies 'take' locally and
no evidence from the water, would be a hackled Gold-
ribbed Hare's Ear or a Pheasant Tail or a Black Spider
or a Greenwell or a Blue Upright fished dry, and a
Pheasant Tail nymph or Tup or Greenwell or March
Brown or Black Spider sunk.

Again, take the local advice. It isn't *always* preju-
diced, ignorant, superstitious, and downright malici-
ous.

In fact, I find that if you behave to the local angler
as you would to a fellow human being, he will soon
come out of his automatic trance of resentment at the
sight of a rival, and will take pride and pleasure in
helping you to fish his favourite water effectively.
There will always be exceptions, of course, but at any
rate the local tackle dealer will find it in his interest to
help you with sincere advice—after all, he wants to sell

you a few flies, to put it at its lowest—*and* he wants you to come again. I have some hundreds of flies which I never really meant to buy, but I don't begrudge the money. It bought more than flies: it bought a bit of local knowledge, and that's a thing you can hardly do without. Mark you, the skilled entomologist who recognises the fly on the water and matches it shrewdly will catch fish anywhere. But what if there is no fly on the water? What do you do then?

(1) Ask the nearest local angler.

(2) If there is no such thing in sight, start off with the flies you happen to like best.

Well, that is a rough résumé of fly fishing on the average river for the average fish by the ordinary methods, and by one method that is by no means ordinary but is the best of the lot. You may find it banned on some waters, where 'one fly only' is the rule. If not—give it a try.

CHAPTER 14

Lake, Loch, and Reservoir

No aspect of angling has changed so radically, over the past decade, as fly fishing for trout in reservoirs. It has been an almost sensational development, opening up new vistas and popularising new techniques and

FIG. 22. Hardy Fresh-water Shrimp.

tackle. I have added a résumé of reservoir techniques at the end of this chapter—the specialist techniques which ingenious anglers have thought up to overcome the specialist difficulties of the crowded, popular waters which have been opened to the angling public recently. But first, a few general observations on still-water fly fishing for trout.

Whether you enjoy lake and loch fishing depends on your temperament. Some anglers are only really happy with moving water: a river has a character of its own, a personality, a *force*. Even if there is nothing doing as regards fish-catching, there is always the murmur and movement of the water, and you can never for a moment forget the mysterious origins of the river and its even more mysterious end in the ocean. Whereas an enclosed sheet of still water is static, relatively dull. I personally find fly fishing just a shade dull on still water—unless, of course, the fish happen to be taking well! I am a poor hand at it, probably because I haven't the right temperament. Well, you will please yourself. It may well be that still-water fly fishing is the only fly fishing available to you, in which case you will probably feel differently about it.

It is probably true that the average weight of trout caught in lakes and reservoirs is greater than the average of all river fish.

Catching them is harder work.

Still-water fly fishing is divided into two very clearly distinguished categories: fishing from the bank, and fishing from a boat. It is further subdivided into all the techniques which you have already heard something about—dry fly, nymph, true wet fly (imitation), and flasher or attractor wet fly.

Generally speaking, dry-fly fishing is not practised so much as sunk-fly fishing—merely because fish are feeding underwater more than on the surface. But the same rules apply.

Boat fishing is delightful or disastrous according to who is doing the rowing. If you are rowing your own boat it is (to me, at any rate) unmitigated hard work without due reward. Not that I mind rowing; but you cannot manage a boat and fish efficiently at the same time. But if you have the services of a character who will provide motive power *and* obey your orders as skipper, you can have a wonderful time. A rower who takes no notice of your wishes, on the other hand, can ruin your day.

An exception to this rule is the really good ghillie, who will take you where the fish are: (*a*) because it pays him to provide you with sport, and (*b*) because he *knows* where the fish are. But if you can afford a really good ghillie you need not have spent the trifle of money on this book, for a really good ghillie will put you wiser than I can. However, it's too late now: no money refunded.

Mark you, there are some terrible bad ghillies: dour, sulky, disappointed old men, stubbornly opinionated (who's talking!), and doggedly rooted in vast stores of misleading myth, abracadabra, empirical mumbo-jumbo, and downright superstition. However, such generally afflict salmon fishers, and we aren't considering salmon fishing just now, but trout.

(Sea-trout fishing in lochs is considered in the chapter devoted to those splendid fish—Chapter 23.)

Your approach to the business of catching trout in still water must be governed by this question of boat or bank. If you are in a boat you can get near to your fish—hence, you have no great need to cast a long line. But if you have to fish from the bank you may have to cast a very long line indeed. Not always. But there are shallow lakes and reservoirs which slope away so gradually that it may be only a few feet deep fifty or a hundred yards from the shore line. Even if you wade—which is usually but by no means universally permitted, *or* desirable—you may still find that to reach feeding fish you have to cast a really good long line. It follows, then, that the bank fisher has to be equipped with somewhat different tools from the boat fisher.

For long casting from the bank, or when wading, you will really need a rod of some nine and a half to ten feet long, butt-actioned, and strong enough to throw about twenty-five yards of line. I should say that that is about the best compromise in outfits. A powerful, stiff, tournament type of rod, though light in the hand and entirely capable of hurling out a prodigious length of heavy line, is not really advisable, in my humble opinion, because: (*a*) it makes fishing real hard work; (*b*) it often involves the use of a too-heavy line in order to bring out the action, whereas you must aim always to get your results with the thinnest line possible; and (*c*) its stiffness makes it really dangerous when striking and playing fish. So on the whole I should recommend a nine-and-a-half- to ten-foot rod with an easy action coming well down to the hand. However, if the necessity for long casting is urgent, then the rod must not be *too* gentle—it must have a certain robustness about it.

Such a tool is still conventional in the sense that it is designed to throw a long double-taper line, or just possibly a weight-forward line. But a radically new approach to the long-casting question has been devised by the new generation of specialist reservoir anglers—the stiff glass-fibre rod, halfway between a fly rod and a spinning rod, if truth be told, which is used to propel a short, heavy 'shooting head' of actual fly line, spliced to a running line of nylon monofilament of about thirty pounds breaking strain. This catapulting action gives prodigious distances, with perhaps a certain amount of loss of control. More details in the section on reservoir fishing at the end of this chapter.

Some few anglers use a double-handed light salmon, grilse, or sea-trout rod for lake fishing. It certainly takes all the hard work out of casting a long line, and I have done it myself over and over again. However, as you will see later, a great deal of your time while fishing a lake with the sunk fly is taken up in recovering the line—and the fly—and this means that the left hand is constantly engaged. This throws the whole weight of the double-handed rod on to the right hand, and not everybody likes that. I personally stick the butt into my tum and find this is a very comfortable way of fishing. Of course, you don't need a whopping great salmon fly rod. A very good compromise, which I'm surprised not to see more widely adopted, is the trout rod with an extension butt—such as the Frank Sawyer 'Still Water' rod made by Farlows, which that great angler William B. Currie has described as 'very nearly the universal' rod. This seems to me the perfect answer. If you feel good and strong, you use it as a single-handed rod. If, like me, you sometimes feel pretty limp, you push on the extention butt and reduce your muscular exertion by about fifty per cent. Such a rod will usually be nine and a half to ten feet long, with an extension butt six inches long.

Against all this, the boat fisher needs only the lightest of rods—eight and a half or nine feet is ample, except in a certain sort of reservoir fishing where you need to sink the fly very deeply—and haul the line up again. For this, you need a stout rod.

Boat or bank, once you have got the mastery of the water you have to fish in exactly the same way. Only the casting mechanics are different.

Some dry-fly fishing is done in still water, but with some notable exceptions (mainly in Wales) most still waters give better sport by far to the wet-fly fisher. For the usual reasons. I should say that lake trout spend about ninety-nine per cent of their feeding time taking underwater food. There are Welsh lakes which are deficient in bottom food but rich in insect life and therefore produce a race of trout that habitually feed on the fly. Here the dry fly is used with success. But, by and large, I assure you, the wet-fly fisher will dominate. It is simple common sense.

It is true that when you see trout working on the surface—and you do—then you may reasonably take them with a dry fly. I have done it many, many times. Especially around weed beds in the evening you may do great execution with a dry fly allowed to rest on the water and very occasionally twitched. But it is not good sense to bother much with the dry fly on the average still water. You do so much better below.

If you see the swirls and rings of rising fish you will naturally tie on a light nymph, grease your leader down to within eighteen inches of the fly, and cast almost as if you were dry-fly fishing for stalked fish. This is terribly exciting. More often, though, you see nothing at all—not a sign of feeding fish. That is when you have to search the water. It is likely that there are always some fish feeding, at *some* level. Your business is to find that level, with the minimum of delay.

Assuming that you are starting to search the water, tie on as long a leader as you dare. Twelve feet is by no means too long—some experts use leaders as long as fourteen feet. But much depends on the wind and the rod and on your skill in casting. If the wind is not too strong, use a good long leader and tie a weighted nymph to the point. Have a dropper about six feet from the point, and on this tie an unweighted nymph of a different kind.

Carefully remove all grease from the nylon with soap or detergent. I carry a little bottle of soapy water, really and truly soapy, a kind of goo. With a scrap of rag, I rub this up and down the leader as needed. Modern synthetic detergents are very good indeed—a little sprinkled on a scrap of wet rag will do the trick. You *must* have a readily-sinking, grease-free leader.

Make your effort and allow the flies to sink as deep as possible. You may have to wait as long as half a minute, but I should say that fifteen to twenty seconds will be enough if your nylon is free from grease and a weighted nymph is helping it down. By this time your flies will be fishing good and deep—but at widely separated levels. Now you begin to give life to the flies by recovering line.

Here we come to the crux of the difference between river fishing and still-water fishing. The moving river inevitably gives a semblance of life even to a rather badly fished fly. (If it did not, bags would be lighter!) But in still water your fly is perfectly inert unless you give it life by giving it motion. (In bad weather when strong winds are blowing other factors intervene to give your fly life. We come to them later.)

Now it is the speed of recovery which matters. Without a shadow of doubt many lake fishermen recover their flies far too fast. Perhaps they are misled by the fact that in river fishing the fly is careering downstream at a great pace. So it is, of course—*but* it moves fast only in relation to the bank: *not* in relation to the water. The fly's speed in relation to the water surrounding it is terribly slow. If you really look into this, by direct observation for yourself, you will see that nymphs move in tiny jerks and darts, and their average speed over a distance of a few yards is really pathetic.

So if you are fishing a true nymph or wet fly, your speed of recovery can hardly be too slow. A tiny pull, a wait, and a tiny pull. My illustrations show one method of gathering up line in the left hand—there are other methods, such as stripping line through, which you learned from the chapter on downstream wet-fly fishing in rivers (Chapter 9). Whichever method you use to recover line—and the one shown here is the neatest and allows the next cast to be made with the minimum of fuss and tangle—the important thing is to *do it more slowly than you would think possible*. If you have made a cast of twenty yards, say, which is a nice one, then you should recover line until you have about six yards out; at that point you must start false casting to get out line again. That means a total recovery of fourteen yards of line. I should say that you ought to take several minutes to recover that amount of line if you are to fish the nymph through the water at something like a natural speed.

If you use a weighted nymph you may actually get it right down on to the bottom. This is a fine thing to aim at, if you can see no sign of feeding fish. When you

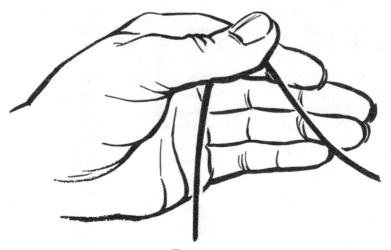

FIG. 23A.

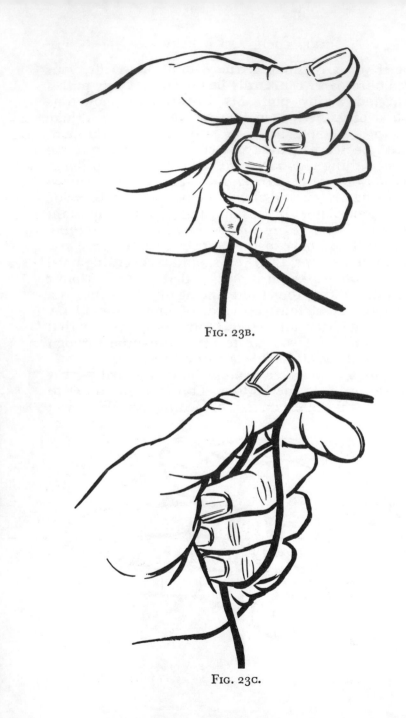

FIG. 23B.

FIG. 23C.

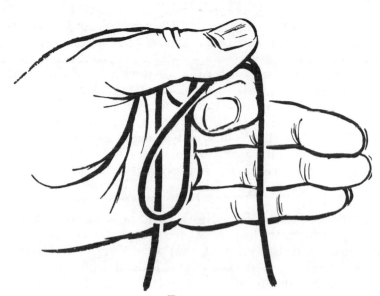

FIG. 23D.

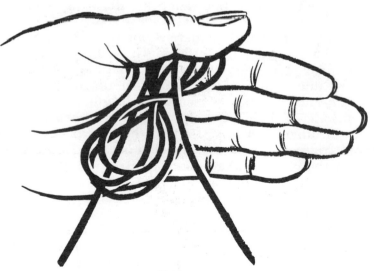

FIG. 23E.
FIGS. 23A, B, C, D and E. Recovering line in the left hand.

116   FLY FISHING

begin to recover line the deeply sunk nymph stirs up the mud slightly and often attracts the attention of a fish.

If you get an early fish on your deep nymph, while it is still deep, you will naturally persevere in fishing at that depth. If, on the other hand, you get a fish on the dropper fly, fishing in mid-water, then you may begin to assume that that is about the right depth at which to fish. In which case you will save a lot of time by replacing the weighted nymph with an unweighted one—or by starting to fish the cast out after a much shorter pause.

I am often asked if the line should be greased, to float, or left ungreased so that it sinks. There are two opinions. I must tell you that many very fine fishers grease the line. It makes it possible, then, to pick the line neatly off the water without much fuss and to make a quick fresh cast to where you may see a fish move. The sunken line takes a lot of hauling up, makes a fuss, and puts a strain on the rods. All of these things are true, and they weigh heavily with some fine fishers.

On the other hand, if there is one thing I abominate more than another in fly fishing it is the greased line that floats. I cannot ever forget that the shadow it throws underwater is prodigious—it throws a shadow like an anchor cable, especially in bright weather and calm water. For this reason, I like to fish when possible with an ungreased line. Despite the drawbacks, I feel more confident then, for the floating line must scare fish. I therefore tend to use a lighter line, ungreased, and softer rod, than most lake fishers.

This means that my distance is reduced, and that is a handicap. I put up with it if I can. On bright, calm, sunny days, anyway, I put up with it. If the surface is broken and rippled by wind, it doesn't matter anything like so much, and then I use a heavier line, floating, and a stronger rod.

I have tried to put the pros and cons fairly. As a

boat fisher by preference, I do not often encounter the problems of bank fishers, who simply have to cast a long line and therefore have to use a heavy line. For boat fishing I like a very light, floppy rod which will cast a line as light as Kingfisher No. 1—and then I never grease it. I can never forget that the champion of champions in the salmon fishing world, the Napoleon of the Wye, Robert Pashley, caught most of his great *salmon* on a thin trout line, ungreased.

This is a foible, perhaps. Most people go armed with a selection of floating and sinking lines, including sinkers which sink at different rates. I am speaking of really serious anglers, you understand!

Most of the flies sold as 'lake flies' have traditionally been attractors, said to resemble fish fry. They *have* to be dragged through the water at speed to give them the slightest semblance of life. Most of them are heavily overdressed, sink reluctantly because they are buoyed up with masses of fur and feather, fish badly, hook badly, and are generally inefficient. Some good lake fishers have long since come to the conclusion that the typical 'lake fly' frightens more fish than it attracts. It is common sense—and highly profitable—to use lightly dressed true nymphs, for that is the fish's staple diet most of the time. Lightly dressed hackle spiders, or true nymphs, fished very slowly on reasonably fine gut, will take most fish. Once you have discovered the whereabouts and the feeding depth of the fish on your given day.

But there are times when the flasher fly will take fish well. At certain times of year—very early in the season, when fish are recovering from the stresses of spawning, and again very late, when they are feeding up for the long lean period—then trout do grab heartily at tiny fish. It is then good sense to offer them the old Butcher, the great Alexandra or Silver Invicta, or other flasher to choice. And, of course, you can try one at any time with some hope of hitting on a bloody-minded fish that feels like a cannibal snack.

The Alexandra has probably caught more lake trout than any other flasher, but as sold in the shops it is usually heavily overdressed and needs half the dressing cut away. A slender, elegantly dressed Alexandra is certainly a fine fly.

When you are fishing the flasher, of course, you have to make it move through the water quite briskly, in darting and erratic movements like a little fish. You cannot very well coil line neatly in the left hand during this operation, and most of us resort to plain stripping, letting the line eventually fall on the ground, or in the boat. (And a great nuisance and peril it is, too.)

On no account, ever, use a flasher and a nymph on the same cast. Only one of them can be fishing properly, for you must fish the attractor fast, the nymph very, very slowly. (Yet I often see the ill-assorted pair teamed together.)

When you have a strongish wind blowing on to the water you may well find that the lee shore provides the best fishing. Fish wait for flies being blown off the land.

The size of your flies is very important. This you must work out either by trial and error (to use two nymphs of different sizes obviously reduces the time spent in finding out) or by local enquiry. If fish are accustomed to nymphs of a certain size they may be quite fastidious on that point (if on no other). If you use only *one* sort of fly, carry it in four sizes.

I believe that a good imitation of the dragonfly nymph should take lake trout, but I don't know of one.

Undoubtedly a wind helps you in lake fishing. When the surface is ruffled your chances of 'getting away with it' are vastly increased. Naturally, it makes your casting problem more complicated, but it pays in other ways. However, don't despair of a flat calm— merely use as fine a leader as you dare, bearing in mind the average size of trout the lake contains. (It is cruelly unsporting to use so fine gut that many fish are sure to be lost, with hooks in their mouths and lengths of gut trailing.)

In a stiff breeze you can make great use of the dropper. You can make it kiss the water, dapping up and down, actually leaving the water if the breeze is strong enough, then sinking a few inches. Meanwhile all your line is in the air. For this rare sport you need a long rod, of course, to give you command over your flies. You use a line of floss silk or nylon floss, knotted every foot or so.

The take of a lake trout is generally decisive, and you rarely need to do anything in the way of striking more active than merely raising the rod.

A boat fisher rarely gathers line in the left hand. He customarily fishes his flies simply by manipulating the tip of the rod, raising it with a slight waggle. Of course, a boat fisher using a shortish line makes very many more casts than a bank fisher. However, it is by no means certain that he *effectively* covers much more water.

When fish are obviously feeding near the surface you may try the old trick of using a dry fly on a dropper and a nymph on the point. Alternatively, of course, a dry fly on the point and a nymph on a *long* dropper, about ten inches long. I am rather fond of this curious combination. You run into a bit of trouble in casting if the dropper gets wrapped about the stem of the main leader, but if all goes well it is a rather attractive way of fishing—especially if there are marked ripples, amounting to wavelets. In such conditions the dry fly rides up and down nicely, and every rise and fall of the dry fly is faithfully reproduced in the sunken nymph. You do not work the flies appreciably, of course—merely a twitch now and again, widely spaced.

Playing a fish in open water is child's play, of course, compared with manoeuvring a strong fish in a snag-infested river. But if a fish dives under the boat you have to be very smart to follow it, putting the rod right underwater if need be. *Never* anchor the boat. If you do, as sure as eggs the fish will take you round the anchor rope. My good old friend Bernard Venables still remembers vividly the day when I nearly lost him a beautiful two-and-a-half pounder at the net through my slowness in getting the drag up. (A drag or drogue, as distinct from an anchor, is permissible; often you simply *have* to use one, if not two, to reduce your speed of drift.)

There is, of course, a very great pleasure to be had merely from being in a boat. I am the last to deny it—the first to proclaim it. However, many otherwise efficient anglers ruin their chances when boat fishing, simply because they can't sit still and won't keep quiet. Voices mean not a thing to the fish, of course—we habitually sing while fishing, my friends and I. But if you knock a pipe out on the gunwale, bang your boots on the bottom, thump oars and things down on the thwarts—then, my friend, you are advertising your hostile presence to the fish in the most clamant way. Vibrations travelling through the water from a boat put paid to any success in that locality for a terrible long time. Row with stealth, too—no 'Boat Race' puddles, no feathering, please.

Essential equipment of the boat angler includes: *warm* clothing—it is always chillier on the water. A hat or sun glasses or both—it is always dazzling when the sun shines. A bailer, used for other and more intimate purposes besides baling out. Plenty to eat, drink, and smoke. A cushion, unless you are naturally well-upholstered.

The usual practice, unless you know something special about feeding localities of the fish, is to row upwind and do a controlled drift down. Then row back *over the same water* and drift down a parallel stretch (of virgin water). You won't usually find the best fish in open water—most of the good 'uns will be taken when casting in towards weeds.

I think that is a fair resumé of ordinary practices on lake or loch. But now let us consider the specialist

techniques developed in recent years by our great
reservoir fly fishers.

Two factors have been chiefly responsible for the big
breakthrough. More and more water undertakings have
been stocking their reservoirs with trout and opening
them to the public—and T. C. Ivens wrote his classic
work, *Still Water Fly Fishing* (Andre Deutsch). With
river fishing for trout steadily becoming either scarcer
or more expensive, or both, the opening up of this new
reservoir fishing has made the sport available to a great
many enthusiasts who might otherwise never have wet
a fly line. One by-product of this development has
been the growth of a school of Midland still-water fly
fishers of great energy, resolution, and ingenuity.
Tom Ivens is their natural leader and high priest, but
others such as the redoubtable Dick Shrive have also
shown the way to do it, and Barrie Welham at Two
Lakes in Hampshire has stalked and caught many
specimen fish.

The high peak of this new fishing may be already
past, but it remains and will always remain a valuable
part of the available sport. Trout that have been
nurtured on the rich feed of newly flooded country are
naturally well fed and enormous when the fishing is at
length opened to the public: some decline follows, but
the level of the fishing remains very high, by river
standards: big brown and rainbow trout are to be had
from these waters, if you learn how to catch them.

There is nothing absolutely radical in the method:
fish are fish for ever, and the essential problem will
always remain the same—how to present to the fish the
fly it wants, at the right depth, without alarming it.
But the special problems of some of these reservoirs
have forced anglers to develop new techniques for
doing just that.

It has been basically a question of attaining the
necessary distance. Some of these waters—perhaps
most of them—are deep in the middle but shallow for
a long way out from the shores. The trout would

naturally feed in the rich shallow verges, but the congregation of anglers taking advantage of this new fishing has been so considerable that the trout quite naturally push off out of the verges and have to be reached out for—*really* reached. One result is that, whereas a good river trout man thinks himself doing well if he casts a genuine twenty yards, or twenty-five at a pinch, a good modern reservoir fisher thinks nothing of thirty-five yards, forty at a pinch. Casts of fifty yards and more, duly authenticated, are not by any means unknown.

Plainly, this sort of distance is unattainable with ordinary river fishing tackle. A tip-actioned rod, that is to say one with a stiff butt and most of the bend in the top half, casts a neat, narrow loop and is good for precise river fishing, but not the right tool at all for this distance work. A butt-actioned rod, one with the graduated bend coming right down to the hand, may make a wider loop but certainly allows you to make a much longer cast, especially with the good old double-taper line. With such a butt-actioned rod, designed by himself, Tom Ivens demonstrated that regular casts of the order of twenty-eight yards were perfectly feasible.

But even this was not enough for the evasive trout of these great sheets of water. What has developed is a form of fly casting that is halfway to spinning. Not every purist fly fisher likes the method, but it is still fly fishing, no question about that, and if it is the only way available to get the fly to the fish, so be it.

The answer seems to be a fibre-glass rod, light but very powerful, with a top joint pretty well as strong as the top joint of a spinning rod. The line is usually a shooting head—some thirty feet of heavy line, either sinking or floating as circumstances and your wishes dictate—spliced to a running line of twenty-five to thirty-pounds breaking strain monofilament nylon. With only the shooting head aerialised beyond the rod tip, and plenty of running line drawn off from the reel, it is a simple matter to send the 'projectile' whistling out a great distance. As I said earlier, it is more like catapulting than casting: but it works, it certainly does.

Tom Ivens has designed several rods for several aspects of reservoir fishing. They are made by Messrs. Davenport & Fordham of 3 Thames Street, Poole, Dorset. The great Dick Walker, an old friend of mine and undoubtedly the most resourceful and inventive of contemporary angling thinkers, has designed a rod made by Hardy's, the 'Walker Fibalite', which will cast anything from a No. 5 line—necessary for fine surface fishing with small nymphs—to a No. 9 shooting head.

Flies that have been conspicuously successful at such waters as Chew Valley, Sutton Bingham, Weir Wood, Grafham, Hollowell, Hanningfield and Ravensthorpe include Mr. Ivens's flasher, the famous Jersey Herd. But the Butcher and a more sparsely dressed version of the good old Alexandra are still in use, successfully— they are indeed immortal—and there are several interesting modern 'minnow' patterns. The Peter Ross will never disappear from fly boxes!

Among the 'deceivers' are the standard nymphs plus a few specially devised for this work (which, incidentally, also work well elsewhere!). They include Tom Ivens's famous Black and Peacock Spider, a wonderfully consistent killer, and a range of nymphs of various colours.

You must never be without imitations of the chironomid—the famous 'buzzer'.

Whether you are stripping line in pretty fast, dragging your flasher through the water to resemble a living organism such as tiny fish fry, or are inching in your delicate nymph, near the surface or near the bottom, you are authentically fly fishing. It isn't everybody's idea of the sport, but the results, in terms of fish, speak for themselves.

CHAPTER 15

Natural and Artificial Flies

There are many successful anglers who never bother much about the identification of the 'fly on the water' and its logical imitation. These are the cheerful gamblers who operate on the principle that 'if a fish is hungry it will take anything that looks like food'—and they are usually right. But there are people who don't like this element of chance, who enjoy knowing exactly what they are *supposed* to be doing: people with a neat, scientific, tidy turn of mind. For these, and for all who want to grow proficient in every branch of their art, I now give a brief summary of most of the natural flies on which trout feed, some idea of when to look for them and how to recognise them—and, most important of all, what artificial to use in order to represent them.

FIG. 24. March Brown nymph and Large Dark Olive nymph.

The March Brown is well described by its name. Unknown on chalk streams (I think), it is the great early fly of the more turbulent rivers of the West. It is a brown fly, big, with chequered wings standing up high, and two tails. The hatch doesn't last long, is very sudden, and usually occurs between 11 a.m. and mid-afternoon.

Artificial: March Brown, both dun (dry) and wet (nymph). The spinner is not imitated.

The Olives are a large family—perhaps the most widespread of the 'bread-and-butter' flies.

First in time comes the Large Dark Olive, hatching at the start of the season. It is closely followed by the Medium Olive, most prolific, perhaps, and most widely imitated and frequently used, of *all* flies.

FIG. 25. Large Dark Olive Dun.

The Large Dark Olive is a dark, bluish-grey fly, with upright, smoky-grey-blue wings, an olive-brown body with darker thorax, and an abdomen ringed by paler bands. Two tails, grey-green. Legs, dark grey and olive.

*Artificial*s: Dun—Blue Upright, Blue Dun, Rough Olive, Dark Olive—or, most popular of all, Greenwell's Glory.

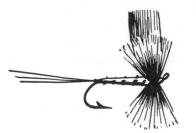 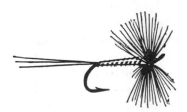

FIG. 26. Greenwell's Glory.   FIG. 27. Blue Upright.

Spinner—the translucent wings of the natural spinner are veined in dark brown, the thorax black, the rest of the body grey.

Artificial: Red Spinner.

The Medium Olive Dun—actually a bit more yellowish than true olive, I often think—is the standard chalk-stream fly, but appears almost everywhere. The dun has smoky-grey wings with a yellow tinge, a brown back and dark thorax, and two grey tails.

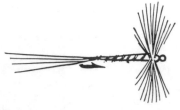　　　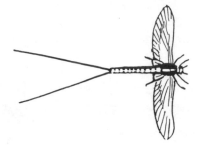

Fig. 28. Red Spinner (imitates the Medium Olive Spinner).　　Fig. 29. Medium Olive Spinner (female).

The artificials to represent the dun are, first and foremost, the great Gold-ribbed Hare's Ear, then Greenwell's Glory, the Olive Quill, or the Medium Olive Dun itself.

Represent the spinner with a smaller version of the Red Spinner than you used to represent the Large Dark Olive Spinner, or, better still, with the Pheasant Tail or with Lunn's Particular. *The Pheasant Tail will serve to represent all the olive spinners* (Mayfly excepted).

A very important fly which starts to appear in May (but often goes on through summer) is the Iron Blue. Trout go mad on it at times. Watch out carefully if you have been catching fish on Medium Olives (or your Gold-ribbed Hare's Ear or your Greenwell) and then you suddenly stop catching fish, though the olives are still hatching. If you have a close look you may well see that the trout have transferred their attentions to a much smaller fly that looks almost black on the water. If you spot this fly, with dark greyish-blue (in fact, iron blue) wings, grey legs, and two grey tails, then switch quickly to an imitation, for trout prefer it, they do indeed. It is a very obliging fly which often hatches in bitter weather (such as we have in May sometimes) and rough, cold, blustery winds. Trout sometimes betray their interest by splashy, excited rises. They go for it so wholeheartedly that the rise-form isn't just a sip and a dimple, the usual neat concentric circles of the spreading ring, but a figure-of-eight whorl made by the whole arching body.

FIG. 30. Iron Blue Dun (natural and artificial).

Artificials: Duns—Iron Blue Dun, Adjutant Blue. Spinner—Pheasant Tail, or that very great fly the Houghton Ruby. (The wet Snipe and Purple makes an effective nymph pattern.)

The Pale Watery Dun is met with from May onwards. A small fly with two tails—about the same size fly as the Iron Blue, but never to be confused. Pale grey wings, pale greenish-yellow body and legs.

Counterfeit the dun with Tup's Indispensable or the Ginger Quill. For the spinner, which in Nature has transparent, veinless wings, try the Tup again, or the Pheasant Tail, or Lunn's Yellow Boy. A good nymph is the wet Tup.

The Blue-winged Olive looks much bigger than the Medium Olive, though really it is not. It has a fatter body and longer wings—high, bluish wings—and *three* tails. The tails of the spinner are much longer than the tails of the dun. The spinners of the B.W.O. (as it is known) have a great peculiarity. Instead of settling on the water singly, like all other female spinners, to deposit their eggs—some crawl down reed

stems to do it—the B.W.O. spinners fly up-river in
great hordes, a real mass attack, and drop their eggs
from the air. They always seem to choose fast water to
deposit their eggs on, so if you have seen a lot of

FIG. 31. Natural and artificial.

Left—Pale Watery Spinner (female).
Right—Pheasant Tail (the correct imitation).

B.W.O. duns and are therefore expecting a fall of
spinners, expect it near fast water. The B.W.O. is an
important *evening* fly.

Artificials: Duns—Orange Quill. *No other.* This
great fact of angling life was discovered by the late Mr.
G. E. M. Skues, the 'inventor' of nymph fishing. Just
that one, the Orange Quill. Imitate the spinner by the
Sherry Spinner or Pheasant Tail.

FIG. 32. Blue-winged Olive Dun (male) and its imitation,
the Orange Quill.

You can easily identify the spinners in flight. They
carry the eggs, in the form of a green ball, clutched
between two lobes at the extremity of the abdomen.
The tails, therefore, point down or actually forward—
they resemble flying ants in this respect.

A great nymph pattern of the Blue-winged Olive is the fly invented by William Law, famous keeper of the Buckland water on the Usk. I am indebted to Captain T. B. Thomas, manager of Milward's, for the information that this pattern—Law's Wet B.W.O.—fished on a short line upstream, is a deadly killer, especially on the Usk. 'A great and certain killer,' says Captain Thomas, in his useful and pleasant booklet, *Trout Fishing Elementary Entomology*. That is recommendation enough for any fly.

FIG. 33. (*Left*) Pale Watery nymph. (*Right*) Mayfly nymph.
(*Hardy Brothers.*)

The Mayfly—surely everybody who has ever been near a river in summer recognises the Mayfly? Biggest of all the ephemerals—twice as big as the Medium Olive, in fact—it has roughly triangular, broad-based wings, pale yellowish-green, with dark veining. Thorax olive and brown, abdomen pale straw colour, with dark markings. Legs brownish-olive; *three* tails, nearly black.

You can take your pick of scores of imitations, both of dun and spinner, and Hardy's for one make a good nymph. (No doubt there are others.) I have long since put aside the winged patterns which look so life-like on the water: they are terrible hookers, owing to the stiffness of the 'wings', and soon get waterlogged. Duns tied with French Partridge hackle, and hackle-point spinners, serve very well. Never mind the colour—the trout surely will not.

The *sedges* have now begun to assume some import-

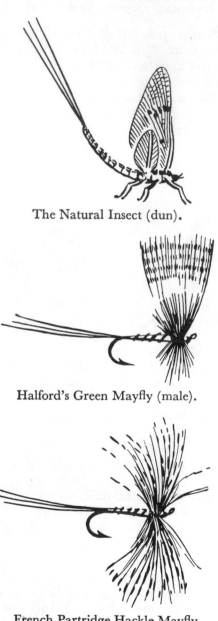

The Natural Insect (dun).

Halford's Green Mayfly (male).

French Partridge Hackle Mayfly.

Fig. 34. Natural and artificial mayflies (duns).

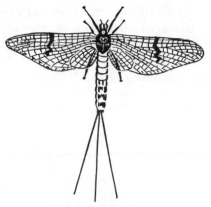

Mayfly Spinner (female).

Mayfly Spinner, Hackle-point Wings.

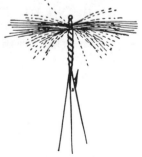

Mayfly Spinner, Henderson Wings.

Fig. 35. Natural and artificial mayflies (spinners).

ance in the angler's life, as summer develops—though
their day is really still to come. The sedges or caddis-
flies are easy to recognise. They have clumsy bodies
and *four* large wings, which have been variously described as being carried (at rest) in 'roof-top' or 'pent-
house' fashion. That is to say, they carry them folded
back with a top ridge and sloping sides, just like a
shallow roof. The Alder looks like a sedge, but its
wings have a sheen, whereas the sedges' wings, being
covered with minute hairs, look dull.

FIG. 36. (*Left*) Alder (natural). (*Right*) Alder (artificial).

Most sedges are nocturnal in habit. The few day-
flying ones include the Caperer, or Welshman's Button
—often a useful fly. Sedges on the water kick up quite
a fuss, and this is the one occasion when a bit of drag
may actually pay. (Certainly it does when fishing in
the dusk.)

Artificials: For the Caperer, which has dark chest-
nut-brown wings, try Lunn's Hackle Caperer or Halford's Welshman's Button. No true nymph, but the
ordinary artificial fished just below the surface will
take when a sedge-fly is on the point of hatching by
bursting out of the larva.

The Alder may be represented by—the Alder. The
Herefordshire Alder is a purplish fly, said to be best
fished wet.

It is later in the year, on hot evenings, that the nocturnal sedge-flies come into their own. Always carry a
leader—quite a stout one—ready mounted with a sedge
pattern, and try it when the light is really going. Often
the biggest fish in the river move then, and only then,

after hiding up all day. A dragging sedge, a sedge cast without finesse, often hooks a really good fish.

Artificials: You may want to represent the Cinnamon Sedge, the Medium Sedge, the Small Dark Sedge, or the Light Sedge. The artificial patterns—for a refreshing change—bear the same names as the natural flies. Isn't that pleasant?

A sedge-fly of importance on some rivers, unknown on others (you see the value of *asking*), is the Grannom. Trout like it when it appears. It is a daytime fly.

FIG. 37. Stone Fly Creeper.

You can always tell it easily. It has a green egg-sac (well, the female has) and the wings are of mottled grey. It appears about late April and early May, when it appears at all. The imitation is simply called the Grannom.

If the Stone Fly appears you may match it with an Orange Partridge. This is a fly of the north. The Willow Fly is also really a Stone Fly—it is a fly easy to know because it is fond of settling on your body and hands! Note the steely sheen of the grey-brown wings. It has an almost invisibly thin, long body and is matched, artificially, by a large Blue Upright tied with a quill body.

When the hawthorn is in bloom you may find the Hawthorn Fly occasionally taken. It is represented by a large Black Gnat.

The ordinary Black Gnat, which starts to appear

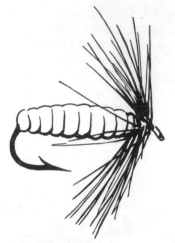

Fig. 38. Caddis Grub.

(often in great quantity) in May, is represented by another easy one—the Black Gnat. If the trout are smutting—that is, sucking in thousands (literally) of tiny reed smuts with their mouths wide open, you haven't much hope, but you can try throwing a Black Gnat with great accuracy right into the fish's mouth.

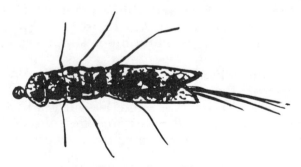

Fig. 39. Stone Fly.

No artificial is tied small enough to represent the smut itself, though people have gone mad trying.

Things fall on the water, from time to time, that have no business there. Trout aren't fussy—they will accept them if they're hungry. These non-aquatic flies include red ants, black ants, and the Black Gnat itself. So carry a couple of Red Ants and Black Ants, but don't waste time putting them up unless you actually see ants in flight and falling on to the water. When trout *do* want them, said the great Halford—when trout find them falling and get the taste of them—then they *really* go for ants. So just keep a couple handy.

FIG. 40. Water Beetle.

High summer has passed with hatches of Pale Wateries, Olives of various sorts, Iron Blues, sedges. Things that are fascinated by water, though they have no business there, have fallen into the river, to be consumed—and imitated by you. September brings, perhaps, heavier hatches of Black Gnat, and all the ephemerals perk up and hatch faster. The Large Dark Olive appears again, and you know the season is almost over.

Make the most of it.

To try to sum up this vast and fascinating subject:

If you want to be reasonably near to Nature but can't be bothered to catch flies and examine them, to memorise patterns, or simply to buy and carry a horde of flies...

The Gold-ribbed Hare's Ear represents the olive duns very well. The Pheasant Tail will ably represent most of the olive spinners—that and Lunn's Particular between them. If trout go solid on the Iron Blue you are more or less sunk without an imitation, an Iron Blue Dun for the dun, a Houghton Ruby or, less certainly, a Pheasant Tail for the spinner.

You need a Ginger Quill for the Blue-winged Olive dun, and a Law's Wet B.W.O. for the hatching nymph. A Tup for the Pale Wateries.

You need Black Gnats, a Caperer, an ant or two, a few sedges.

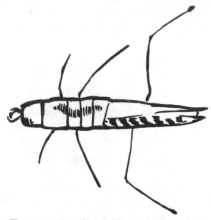

FIG. 41. Artificial 'Grasshopper'.

But if you must go even farther in simplification, then I would say that for average decent fishing on most rivers, the Blue Upright for the duns and the Pheasant Tail for the spinners are the real great stand-by favourites. With those two you can get along—and plenty of nymphs.

Myself, I should unhesitatingly substitute the Gold-ribbed Hare's Ear for the Blue Upright. But most people would not. I just happen to have great faith in it. Some would use a Greenwell's Glory in place of both.

Never forget this. It is true, sometimes, that trout go for one fly to the temporary exclusion of all others. It is true that they get used to certain flies at certain times of year. Yes. *But*—don't worry overmuch about exact imitation. Present a fly that looks eatable. Few fish will ignore it, by and large, even though it be out of season.

CHAPTER 16

The Mayfly Carnival

Some waters breed no Mayfly. On others, this enormous and beautiful fly hatches in countless millions. Where there is a hatch of Mayfly, there is invariably tremendous and contagious excitement.

There is an old belief that Mayfly time is the 'duffer's fortnight' or 'duffer's paradise'. Apart from being unkind, this is also untrue. It is true that during the Mayfly season there is usually *a chance* of making bigger and better bags than at any other time. It is true that the biggest fish in the water, which remain unseen and unsuspected for the rest of the year, feeding steadily on the bottom, come up to take this great succulent mouthful. Yes. But it is also true that the Mayfly season can easily provide the biggest disappointments and humiliations of the entire year.

However, most of us would not like to miss a go during Mayfly time.

The Mayfly nymph does not cling to stones or weeds or twigs. It burrows quite deep into silt and mud. It has a comparatively robust outer husk or shuck (which trout seem to like).

The hatch begins as early as mid-May (hence the name), but on some waters it does not begin until June. The entire season runs from mid-May (at the earliest) to about mid-June. On any water, except some of the Irish loughs, which have fantastic Mayfly seasons, it lasts for about a fortnight.

At first no fish seem to notice the Mayflies hatching. Then the smaller fish, wildly excited, start to have a go at them—their wild, splashy, often inaccurate, and probably nervous rises to these big flies sound unlike any other rises whatever. Later the bigger fish cotton on to it, and begin to suck down the duns with less fuss but no less determination. The biggest fish in the water join in. You feel that you cannot possibly go wrong, as you see the water come alive with rising fish, and hatching flies everywhere.

But you *can*. You can go badly wrong.

You can find your artificial being ignored by fish that are steadily rising to natural flies within inches of yours.

The bigger and better the hatch, in fact, the worse you are likely to do. Some anglers loathe the Mayfly Carnival precisely because there is so much competition from natural flies that the poor old artificial stands a poor chance of being chosen.

I can give only two pieces of advice. First, try to get in early, within the first few days, before the fish have become sated with natural fly, before the natural fly has become too plentiful. Secondly, use the nymph.

Frequently, when a fish, seen to be steadily feeding (as you think) on the hatching dun, refuses your well-placed artificial, you can take that fish on a nymph sunk only *just* below the surface, on a greased cast. The fact is that the trout enjoy the shuck out of which the dun hatches—it is a mouthful much to their taste—and the fish which you thought was concentrating on duns may well have been concentrating on duns just at that moment when they were struggling out of the shuck.

I fish the nymph with zeal, believing it to be an on-the-whole better bet than the dun.

Later in the Carnival, after about a week, the great mating dances take place. The males, having shed a coat and emerged in all their translucent finery, undulate up and down in the air—hence the term dance—awaiting the females. As soon as a female appears several males dart after her. One seizes her, they mate, dropping into the grass. The fertilised female, now a *spinner*, flies to the water, ever flying upstream, to deposit her eggs. Having laid them on the surface, her wings sink down flat and she floats along, dead.

Now is the time when you can count on real sport. The so-called 'Spent Gnat' (an absurd misnomer) is a taking fly. Better than the hatching dun, if for only one reason. That reason is that the hatching dun is struggling on the water—and no artificial can reproduce that movement. Whereas the spent fly *is* spent, is lifeless and inert; and that is a condition which the artificial fly *can* reproduce.

But when there is a fall of spinners there may also be a hatch of duns—and it *may* be, though not certainly, that the trout will be concentrating on the one or the other. You must look carefully at the water to ascertain if this is so—otherwise you may be wasting your time by offering them a dun, say, when they are preferring spinners. Or the other way round. It is failure to do this that costs many anglers good sport, and some their reason.

Fortunately they are easily identifiable. The duns are actually darker, seen against the light, but *on the water* they look lighter, and the spinners, even before their wings fall flat, look somewhat grubby, darkish. Of course, when the spinner lets her wings fall flat in the moment of death, she becomes unmistakable. Note carefully if the trout are favouring the one or the other. It may make all the difference to your sport.

Despite the undoubted uncertainties and disappointments of the Mayfly season, it does bring up trout of a size which you would swear never existed in the water. It is therefore quite irresistible to the average angler, who sees few enough good trout. All I can say is—use the nymph freely, and watch for evidence that trout are discriminating between spinner and hatching dun.

Your tackle should present no difficulties, but, of course, you must use stouter leaders than you would normally tie on. It isn't only the chance of an outsize fish which makes this imperative: it is the effort of carrying a big fly, several times bigger and heavier than usual. On a fragile leader such a fly is an actual menace. You must use a reasonable gauge of gut or nylon—not less than 2X, I should say, and 1X if you know that the water holds numbers of big fish. The big fly will soon weaken fine stuff at the 'hinge'. Another point: it takes extra power to pull in the rank barb of a big hook. In fact, you just can't do it with fine gut: even if the fly does not fatally weaken the gut in the act of casting, your chances of breaking when you strike (not to mention being broken during the fight) are unduly high. And, of course, there's no point in leaving a hook in a fish.

Some well-to-do anglers use a stouter rod altogether during the Mayfly festival, but I don't think it's necessary. Though big, with plenty of wind resistance, the Mayfly is not actually very heavy, in the sense that a salmon fly has real weight. You need strong nylon, true, but the rod top of any ordinarily good trout rod will stand up to a few hours of Mayfly slinging without protest. However, I must admit that a really gentle wet-fly rod of the kind I like to use myself is *not* the best tool for this job.

As to imitations, they are legion. The big-winged Mayfly still finds some supporters, but, though it looks pleasantly 'real' floating down the stream, it rapidly becomes waterlogged, and the enormous mass of stiff wing makes it a very bad hooker. Far, far better to use the soft-hackled fly—particularly, I think, the French Partridge hackle fly. It sits lightly on the water, is beautifully gauzy and translucent against the light, and the soft hackle means that the fish has less trouble in getting this outsize mouthful well and truly en-gulfed.

Naturally, you are in no hurry to strike when Mayfly fishing—even less of a hurry than at other times. (And the dry-fly man should *never* strike abruptly.) A Mayfly is a lot for a fish to get hold of. True it is that it is easily recognised to be a fake and quickly repudiated —but if it is difficult to get hold of, it is likewise not too easy to spit out. Anyway, the fact is that you must give the fish plenty of time to turn downwards with the fly in his mouth before you set the hook. On the other hand, it is a lot of hook to set, so when you *do* strike, make a job of it. Not a panicky strike, of course, not a wild strike; but this is one time when your upwards movement should be decisive and quite strong.

I mentioned that tremendous hatches of Mayfly take place regularly on some Irish loughs. Dapping is the favourite way of seducing such fish during the Mayfly season (see Dapping: Chapter 21). It is true, also, that you can sometimes dap a Mayfly successfully from behind a tree or bush on our rivers.

Another point I want to make is that often the merest bit of a brook or ditch has a hatch of Mayfly— and then, believe me, if you creep along with an artificial you may get an outsize surprise.

CHAPTER 17

Brook Fishing

Brook fishing is for the indefatigable, the impecunious, and the uncorrupted. It appeals powerfully to the many who have a strong taste for the miniature. It is consoling and charming, fruitful and strenuous, fascinating and cheap.

I must admit that big rivers appeal to me very strongly, making an insistent call to something primeval, perhaps, in my imperfectly understood temper. At least once in a year I must wade deep into a big river and surrender to its pull. But the attraction of opposites is strong. Brook fishing presents all the problems and all the attractions of big-river fishing, scaled down to a manageable size. It has, also, charms of its very own.

There are at least two sorts of brook fishing. There is the open, windswept, rather barren and austere brook fishing of moorland and mountain, and there is the tangled, close-grown 'ditch' fishing of farmland and valley. They present different problems, and the atmosphere of the one is quite unlike the atmosphere of the other.

Both sorts of brook fishing have this in common: they demand skill, extreme caution and self-effacement, and animal stealth. They also, as a rule, produce a race of very small fish with occasional gratifying whoppers.

The term whopper is relative, of course. When you get into a half-pounder on a water that customarily produces trout running six to the pound, that is a red-letter day. All the upland brooks tend to be spare, bare, swift; not well supplied with natural food, and therefore prone to nurture a race of hardy, half-

starved, ravenous little chaps. But even in these there
is always, lurking in some relatively deep hole, a half-
pound monster.

The position in the 'ditch fishing' country is somewhat different. Almost everywhere you go in Britain
you can find lowland ditches, sometimes no more than
a few feet wide, meandering sluggishly through the
pasture land. They contain fish far oftener than is
generally thought, and although the fish may be few,
they suffer no lack of natural food and tend to run to
surprising weights.

I greatly enjoy a day on the moors, fishing for the
many little red-spotted trout and hoping for the rare
big 'un. But wherever I happen to be staying, I make a
point of looking out for the sluggish ditch flowing
through fat farmland. You will as often get a derisive
smile as you will get permission to fish such a pill; but
have a care—if fish have ever been introduced to such
neglected waters, and if the water is free from pollution, then there will be fish in the water still, and often
surprisingly fat, sturdy fish, too. For such slow drains
teem with food for fish, and are generally almost un-
fishable and quite unfished.

The perfect gear for what the Scots call 'burn fishing' is a trifling little wand of a rod; six feet long is
plenty, seven feet may seem all too long. With it you
will use a fine line and a two-yard leader of gut or nylon
tapering to 4X at the stoutest. For a long time, until it
was irretrievably 'borrowed', I used the top joint of a
very old fifteen-feet-long greenheart grilse or sea-trout
rod, stuck into a short handle of my own manufacture.
It made a delicate little tool less than six feet long,
with which one could switch the light line into every
eddy and under every bush.

For you need to do a lot of crafty switching and
searching. Brook trout may be hungry, but they are
not fearless. If they become aware of your presence,
fear will conquer hunger. You must use extreme
stealth. Two factors militate against success in the fish-

ing of moorland streams: first, the lack of cover which is characteristic of that sort of landscape, and second, the quaking, boggy ground which often accompanies brook-sides. There are innumerable upland brooks which literally cannot be approached without giving the fish warning, simply because the banks are undercut by floods and the ground trembles at your footstep —thereby sending out waves of vibration which warn the fish, who scuttle to cover.

There are two ways of going about this problem. You can adopt the bold line and get right into the water, or you can stay as far away from the water's edge as you think necessary in order to avoid warning the fish. Whichever way you take, you will find it exciting fishing.

The wader, once in, is committed. Having entered the water, you stand absolutely still until the alarm of your entry has died down. Fortunately for anglers, fish soon forget. Then you begin to make your way upstream, step by careful step. You cannot move too carefully, or too silently. Move with the stealth of a burglar on the stairs. Make no wave. Put your feet down as if on a creaking board.

I exaggerate not. If you go breasting the stream, sending out a wave-warning ahead and tramping heavily on the gravel bed, you alert every fish for yards upstream. The process is cumulative: you will be ready to swear that the stream is fishless. However, if you move with perfect stealth you will pick up fish all the way upstream.

The wading upstream angler is a dry-fly man, as a rule. He is standing 'behind' the fish—which, of course, have their heads pointing upstream and are unaware of him. He pitches his fly upstream and slightly to right or left. He lets it ride down on the current until it is practically at his feet. Then he whips it neatly off the water, makes a fuss-free horizontal false cast or two to dry it, and pitches it upstream again.

Most of his fish he will pick up on the edges of the
stream. They cannot afford to squander energy by
lying in the force of the current. Trout will always be
found lying where they can get at the food which the
current brings down with the minimum expenditure
of energy.

That is why an eddy, or a deep hole, is usually in-
habited by the best fish in the water. A rock, an out-
jutting root, or mere configuration of bed or bank,
often produces a situation highly agreeable to trout.
Especially an eddy, where a fish may lie in comfort, out
of the force of the stream, yet able to pick up drowned
flies as they swirl slowly round and round in the relatively still, quiet, often scummy water. These are spots
which the brook fisher learns to exploit.

I have said that the upstream brook fisher is, at least
as often as not, a dry-fly man. This has become true in
recent years, but not so very long ago the wet fly was
almost the only lure used by fly fishers who haunted
the swift, rocky streams of upland and moorland. The
vogue for fishing the floater even in fast, broken water
is a recent one. It works, and it is by far the easiest
method. Therefore you should know of it. But it is
not, in fact, the most effective method. Not in my
opinion, that is. I would back the wet fly, fished upstream, to beat the dry fly every time in *numbers*,
though not necessarily in quality and size of fish taken.

The downstream wet fly is unthinkable on such
water: you would scare every fish away. The only
exception to this rule is the 'overland' cast which drops
most of the line on dry land and just a yard or two,
plus cast and fly, in the water. If you possess only one
rod, and that too long for true casting on a brook, then
this is your answer.

CHAPTER 18

Grayling

The grayling occupies a rather anomalous position in the man-proposed hierarchy of fishes. Game fishers of a highly discerning cast of mind, who recognise only members of the salmonidae family as fish, grudgingly admit the existence of the grayling: for, indeed, the grayling *is* a member of that august and very well-connected family. Who but biologists and snobs care? However, game fishers are not really whole-hearted about the grayling: it is nearly a game fish, but not quite. Coarse fishers welcome him more warmly: to the confirmed maggot-trotter he is game all through and entirely acceptable.

To a sensible all-round angler who takes the natural world as he finds it, a grayling is a grayling is a grayling. With warm regards to Miss Gertrude Stein. A very fine fish indeed, sporting to a degree, palatable, and extremely obliging.

Miss Stein would not know it, but the grayling is known by other names. *Umber*, they call him in the north, and for that matter elsewhere: umber, the shadow. The grey shadow of the stream. 'Silver Lady' and 'Lady of the Stream', the more whimsical brethren assert; though since the grayling is as often male as female, it seems a shade twee to label it feminine. 'Thymallus' is the official name, allegedly bestowed because a fresh-caught grayling smells faintly of thyme. I haven't actually met an angler who has noticed this, and I haven't noticed it myself. But undoubtedly the fresh-caught grayling *does* have a faint and perplexing odour—a whiff of cucumber, some say—which is un-like the scent of any other fish. No matter. (Scrape off the scales before you cook a grayling, or you *will* notice a faint, unsettling odour.)

What matters, to us, is that the grayling rises freely
to the fly exactly when trout are out of season. Spawning about the same time as the coarse fish, in early
spring, the grayling strengthens up during summer
and is fighting fit by autumn, just when the trout are
going to spawn. After a frost or two, and right through
the winter, if it be not too turbulent, the grayling is in
perfect order. You see that if there are grayling available to you you can go on fly fishing right through the
year, or at least for ten months of it. Bless the grayling.

Purists tend not to bless it, holding that grayling are
vermin which eat food that trout should take, and
even that they bully trout and thrive strictly at the
trout's expense. (But then, to the purist all things are
impure.) Owners of trout streams often persecute the
grayling as if they were pike. Since I own no water, the
problem has not presented itself to me in an acute
form. I am always glad to know that there are grayling
anywhere, for then I go on using the fly rod through
the otherwise intolerable months when fly fishing is
not to be had. In fact, trout bully grayling.

'Grey shadow of the stream' is a fair description of
the grayling. But when you look at a fresh-caught fish,
you see that underneath the overall silver-grey hue
lurk fleeting rainbow colours, soon to fade, of the most
exquisite beauty: blue, white, gold, and through the
red scale from pink to purple. A lovely fish indeed.

Apart from the variation in spawning times, the
chief distinction between trout and grayling is that the
latter do not, even when food-conscious, lie poised
high in the water. The grayling is distinguished by a
huge, powerful dorsal fin and by a singularly large air-
bladder. This equipment, plus remarkable eyesight,
enables the grayling to lie on the bed of the stream
and to rise almost vertically to take a fly from the surface. This arrangement makes fly fishing for grayling
quite different from fly fishing for trout.

Not in respect of tackle—or, indeed, flies, though of
that, more later—but in the manner in which you

approach the fish. When you know (or suspect) that grayling are present you can fish a dry fly on the stillest dead water, fairly deep water, which would be pretty hopeless for trout, in the expectation that any moment a grey shadow will lunge up from the depths at lightning speed, seize your fly, and plunge down again all in one movement. This makes dry-fly fishing for grayling enormously exciting—and since you have to use very fine gut, and since the grayling usually hooks itself in that downward plunge, you have to have fairly good 'hands' to avoid breaks if the fish run fairly large. They often do.

This is the chief peculiarity of the grayling—this odd habit of rising almost vertically from bottom to surface, and immediately plunging down again. But there is another point, more or less implicit in the first. It is obvious that the grayling has very fine vision at long range—it is, in fact, a long-sighted fish. But it becomes equally obvious that the excellence of long-range vision is balanced by a corresponding deficiency in close-range sight. In fact, the grayling is a fish that needs bifocals. Time and again a grayling will miss your fly completely. It can be annoying.

However, you never need strike a grayling when dry-fly fishing. If it *does* get your fly it will surely hook itself on the downward plunge before you are awake to what is going on.

Grayling tend to go in shoals. They are rather exceptionally gregarious, among the game fish. If you take one, you can profitably fish that spot in the hope and expectation of taking others. A run which might yield you one or at most two trout may well produce half a dozen grayling. Once you have found the fish, stick it—for the shoals are apt to be fairly widely distributed, with much grayling-free water between them.

In summer, when grayling are just beginning to pick up from the effects of spawning, you can look for them (that is, if you *must* fish for them in summer: it's rather unfair and you get a poorly-conditioned fish) just below runs of fast water. They tend to lie out of the current in deep holes; well, not deep, but deep in relation to the fast runs immediately upstream. Here they get well-oxygenated water, essential for recovery, plus some measure of ease.

In autumn, the exciting autumn, grayling come out on to the shallows and provide tremendous sport in fast, shallow water—my own favourite kind of fishing, for there is the appearance of activity even when 'nothing doing' is the order of the day from the strict fish-catching point of view.

Winter generally finds grayling in the deeps, especially in dead still, deep runs over clean, gravelly bottoms. This is pre-eminently the time for the speculative floating fly.

It is fairly widely believed that grayling are very susceptible to a touch of red in the fly—the famous Red Tag is the grayling fly *par excellence*. No doubt there is some truth in this, but probably it is no more true of grayling than of any other fish. Red and black, it is notorious, are fine colours in flies, any flies, for any fish.

Red Tag, Red Spinner, Red Ant, Red (or Soldier) Palmer, red-tipped black Zulu, Black Spider, Black Gnat, Iron Blue Dun, Tup, and Greenwell's Glory have all done great execution among the grayling. I have caught them on a Wickham's Fancy.

One important thing to remember is that grayling like their dry flies small. Small flies, therefore very fine leader-points. It makes grayling fishing a delicate and satisfying pastime.

Wet-fly fishing for grayling differs from trouting in another important respect. Grayling are not fish-eating carnivores, and are rarely taken on a spinner. It follows that the flasher flies which represent fish fry are not much used in grayling fishing. You have to stick to fly imitations—and nymphal imitations, of course.

This more or less rules out the old across-and-downstream method, which comes into its own mainly when flashers are on the cast. I say 'more or less' because I *have* known cases of grayling taking a sunk fly on the turn, as it began to be dragged across the current. I recollect great execution being done with a fresh-water shrimp imitation on the lower Itchen, fished across and down and invariably taken with a bang just when it began to drag across the stream. But I can only think this was rather exceptional. In my personal experience, it is advisable to fish the sunk fly upstream, obliquely, as one would for trout.

There is never any need to sink your wet flies deeply; the grayling's obliging habit of rising a great way sees to that. I normally fish with a greased line, and my flies (two at most, usually just the one on the point) are seldom sunk more than a few inches. This makes for interesting fishing, since one almost always sees the actual rise.

Any kind of small nymph tied on 4X—5X if you trust your hands and nerves—or a small, sparsely-hackled spider, reds and blacks predominating, will serve to attract grayling when they are in the mood to be attracted. Fortunately, this is often—except, of course, on those awful east-wind days when everything seems dead, river and fish included. They *do* occur, you know. Be prepared.

By and large, however, the grayling can be counted on to provide good sport. A crisp winter's day, with bright, cold sunshine sparkling on the water after a cold night is often memorable to the grayling fisher.

I mentioned earlier that confirmed trotters of the blue-bottle maggot have a soft spot for grayling. Fly fishers, too, especially in the north of England, are somewhat prone to impale a maggot on the point of the fly hook. I never take to this practice myself, but I don't really know why. It seems a bogus form of fly fishing, I suppose. However, it is the best way of presenting a maggot to a grayling at a depth of only a few inches. You will please yourself.

Never forget the tip of using a fly with a bit of wash-leather tied in at the tail ...

I found the translucent plastic-bodied nymphs as made by the late George King, of Kingsmills, Elgin, Morayshire, extremely effective. Perhaps they simulated the true nymph better than other means.

The kind of fly which, instead of laying its eggs on the surface, swims down underwater and crawls down stems of weed, always attracts grayling. It is represented by any small, waterlogged fly, thoroughly sucked to make sure it sinks. Such a fly is the better if the hackles have been clipped.

All in all, the grayling is a great fish for the fly fisherman, his stand-by in winter and ever his delight.

CHAPTER 19

Salt-water Fly Fishing

I carefully say 'salt water' instead of 'sea', because in fact there is no great amount of fly fishing done in the open sea itself, but a certain amount in the salt water of estuaries and close inshore. It is still, I think, the exception rather than the rule to see a man fly fishing in salt water, but those who *do* have a great deal of fun and catch plenty of fish.

Great numbers of fish are caught every year, even in the open sea, on 'feathers'. This is really a debased form of fly fishing, inasmuch as the lure is made on exactly the same principles as a wet fly—that is to say, it consists of feathers or hackles whipped to a hook, and when moved in the water it roughly represents a small fish, or a shrimp. The essence of fly fishing is there, you see. But 'feather' fishers, as a rule, rig up a dozen or so lures on a stout hand-line with a heavy weight at the end of it. They pay out line until the array of feather lures is working deep enough—sometimes right on the bottom—and then jig them up and down, by hand. You can hardly call that fly fishing, can you? Yet immense numbers of fish are regularly taken, by professionals, on 'the feathers'. It is proof conclusive that feather and hair lures—*'flies'*, that is—really do work, and an obvious invitation to the sporting angler to pursue the matter farther, with appropriate gear.

I am particularly fond of this practice, not from any vague aesthetic motive and certainly not for any quasi-ethical reason, but simply because organic baits are messy and often hard to find just when you need them most. At such times fly fishing or spinning appeals strongly. I must confess that I often combine the two practices, and *spin* with a *fly*.

Once you have seen a 'fly' of the kind generally considered suitable for sea fishing you will understand. It isn't, as a rule, the delicate little bit of fluff which you use in streams and lakes. The standard 'sea fly' is a fairly monstrous creation, consisting of feathers dyed in the brightest colours, whipped to stout, long-shanked hooks, and sometimes, though not always, decorated with tinsel and hackles around the body. It often

FIG. 42. Three-hooked 'Terror'.

measures three inches long, occasionally more: and since it is taken to represent a small fish, or an eel, that is fairly reasonable. But it is a devil of a contraption to cast with a fly rod. Nothing short of a stoutish double-handed salmon fly rod will throw a lure as big as that. Not for long, anyway.

In fact, sea fishing can be practised with quite small flies, quite successfully. But the huge feathery creations *do* work, surpassingly well on occasion, and so do bucktails and streamers, sometimes with weighted heads. To put out lures of this nature, I unreservedly recommend the use of a light (trout-sized) spinning rod and a threadline reel. There is nothing to touch this combination, especially if you are fishing from a boat, when the shortness of the rod is a help, instead of a hindrance.

Would you call that fly fishing? But of course! The lure can only be categorised as a fly—if a salmon fly is accepted as a fly, a sea lure is certainly, and equally, a fly. (By the way, big salmon flies work exceedingly well in the sea. But since they practically come into the category of fine arts, and cost up to £1 apiece, you probably won't be exposing them to the ruinous effects of salt water. No. I agree. But have you thought of this situation *the other way round*? Why not try something as cheap and simple as a 'sea fly' for salmon? Oh yes, it

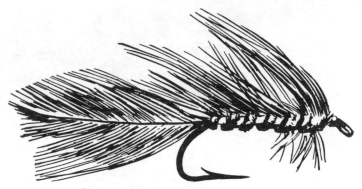

FIG. 43. Hardy's 'Matuka' Lure.

does work, at least it does sometimes. I have seen three salmon one after the other come savagely to a 'sea fly' three inches long, consisting of ordinary brown rooster feathers tied on a slender tube of Systoflex electrical conduit, with the trace passed through it and a small treble tied on the end.)

However that may be—and anything that reduces the expense of salmon fishing is worth investigation—big traditional sea 'flies' are well worth using, and unless you have a strong salmon fly rod to throw them, the best bet is to cast them from a fixed-spool reel. A hybrid version of fly fishing, yes; but fly fishing, nevertheless. Using a light tubular glass trout spinning rod and nylon monofilament of about two and a half or three pounds breaking strain, you can have the

greatest fun catching bass streaking up the estuary
nearly on the surface, and as for mackerel, they fight to
take the lure, at times.

If you wish to use true fly fishing gear, then you will
need a rod rather stouter than would serve for trout
fishing. It has to be strong, not because the fish habitually run to rod-smashing weights, but because of the
strain of picking up a heavy lure and a drowned line
time and again and throwing them backwards and forwards. The big sea flies can only safely be fished with a
strong salmon rod, as I said. The smaller lures can be
cast with a single-handed, strongish rod, what would
usually be called a sea-trout rod. Even so, I am inclined to recommend a double-handed rod all the time.
It makes life a very great deal easier, though a bit of a
nuisance, not to say peril, in a dinghy. Casting fifteen
or to twenty-five yards with a double-handed rod is
child's play; but make the cast a few hundred times
with a ten-foot single-handed rod and you will feel you
have been working for a blacksmith as striker! The
best rod for this purpose, I should say, would be a
twelve-foot tubular glass rod, which is practically indestructible and perfectly impervious to the corroding
action of salt air and water.

The line used to be a problem for the salt-water fly
fisher, but is a problem no longer. The modern plastic
line is pretty well corrosion-proof.

Although I recommended the use of a trout-size
spinning rod for the big feather lures and streamers, I
must point out that the spinning rod is useless for
throwing an ordinary small fly—unless you follow the
late Alexander Wanless's advice and use a float. If you
use a transparent bubble float, partly filled with water,
you get the necessary weight for casting, all right, and
undoubtedly you can catch fish. But I don't care much
for the dragging weight of the heavy bubble when fishing a small fly in tidal water, and in such circumstances prefer the fly rod proper. I am hardly a purist,
as you will have divined already; but by the time you

have fixed yourself up with a spinning reel and a float, you have lost touch with fly fishing, whatever the nature of your lure. However, I mention it since you may feel no such qualms, and I admit they are indefensible; it's just a matter of taste.

Fishing an estuary—which is perhaps the most profitable sphere of operations for the salt-water fly fisher—is exactly like fishing the downstream wet fly for trout. That is to say, you cast directly across the current and let the tide (making or receding) swing your line and lure round until it lies directly downstream of you, when you recover it in the usual way. You search slack water at bends, the vicinity of rocks and weeds—or any place where you suspect fish to be feeding near the surface.

Needless to say, you take some pains to discover the most profitable places to fish. My own salt-water fly fishing has been confined to bass and mackerel, and it is probably safe to say that they are the commonest fish taken on the feathered lure. You learn, by diligent observation and polite questioning, the habits of the fish. You find out where they tend to run—there are often especially good channels and normally barren channels—and there you station yourself. Wherever you see birds diving or making a fuss, wherever you see small fry leaping in an effort to escape their pursuers—those are spots to fish. Naturally, I can make only the most general observation for you: your own acute local observation will put you on to the right spots.

Very often, when fishing my favourite estuary, we see the bass streaking in right on top of the water, cutting it with their dorsals. They are then practically uncatchable by any means except the fly. Later, when the tide is running out, they seem to return to sea deeper, much deeper, in the water, and we have had little luck with feathered lures, or spinners, but have taken sea-bound fish with ragworm and fish baits. It pays to be well armed and to experiment almost ceaselessly.

I am told that mullet, those most difficult, velvety fish, may be taken on a small fly delicately cast. I hope that it is true, and must try one day. Herring can be caught from a boat when they come inshore; so can billet, small coalfish and pollack, shad and garfish. Ordinary river trout wet flies may be used with hope of success, but feather streamers are better.

CHAPTER 20

Coarse Fish on the Fly

Coarse-fish anglers—'bottom fishers', as they are inelegantly called—are a knowledgeable breed of hardy and patient men. But the addicts of the float and bait miss a good deal of fun, I always think, if they stick stubbornly to their traditional gear and never cast a fly to lure their favourite quarry.

For, of course, fly fishing is by no means merely or exclusively a method of angling for the aristocratic game fish, the salmonidae. There are probably very few species of fish which do not at some time or another take a caddis or a nymph to supplement their diet. I don't say that they may all be caught by the fly fisher, but the following species definitely can, and provide great sport: chub, dace, rudd, roach, perch, pike.

I have put them in the order of accessibility, more or less. Thus, few perch and vastly fewer pike are ever caught on the fly—though more would be taken if more anglers tried. Dace and chub are ever-willing takers, rudd will frequently oblige, and roach sometimes; it depends largely on the water they inhabit.

The chub really is a most obliging fish. He feeds in the heat of a summer's day when all other fish, except perhaps the equally voracious little gudgeon, are disinclined to stir. He is equally, or almost equally, willing to oblige at the other end of the temperature scale, when the water is so cold that most fish are too lethargic to care. And at all points in between.

He takes cherries, cheese, snails, bread, worms, minnows, shrimps, bacon rind, bootlaces, berries—just about the most catholic appetite of them all. He obliges the bottom fisher, the spinner, the man who angles with a float, the long-trotter, the leger-keeper, the spinner, and the fly fisher. What a noble fish is the chub!

He grows large, too—a two-pounder is nothing to talk about, a five-pounder is merely respectable. The only faults to which the chub must plead guilty are that he is almost uncatable, and that though satisfactorily greedy, he has no great fighting heart and is inclined to give up the struggle after one terrified dash for the safety of his lair.

Fly fishing for chub is essentially a summer pursuit. It is in summer that the chub, usually in shoals, for they are gregarious fish, saunter up and down a strictly defined short beat, usually under overhanging trees, on the lookout for choice morsels, such as fat caterpillars, which drop from the trees. It is this proclivity of the chub for caterpillar-snatching which has given rise to the belief that there is such a thing as a special 'chub fly'—a fuzzy monstrosity of a Palmer, red or brown or black, tied with innumerable turns of hackle round the body.

Well, it is true enough that a chub will take a 'chub fly', properly presented. But a chub will take almost *any* fly, properly presented. Be it a true nymph, a spider, a dry fly of any species you care to name, or a sunken flasher, such as the Butcher, which represents fish fry. The chub is as catholic in his taste for flies as in his taste for any other form of fish food.

I suppose *most* fly fishing for chub consists of flicking a fly underneath overhanging branches of water-side trees, for that is where chub are oftenest to be found—in the slack water near the bank, within a yard or so of the bank. A very fine way of going about it is to drift silently downstream in a canoe or dinghy and flick your fly in under the branches wherever you see them hanging out over the water. Preferably you have a friend with you to manage the canoe. However, if a boat is not available, and you have to fish from the bank, things can be rather more difficult.

Once you have located the chub under the trees
your problem is to get the fly to them without your
presence being suspected. Chub are by no means shy of
tackle, but they are very alert to the presence of
human beings, and if your heavy tread on the bank
scares them—or if they catch sight of you—they will
simply disappear, sinking silently down out of sight
without apparent effort or panic. You can, of course,
try the drift downstream from a position above, as
described earlier for trout; but remember—you have
only one shot. It is almost a certainty that in picking
your fly and line off the water at the end of a drift, you
will put the fish down.

Another—perhaps the commonest—way of tackling
this problem is to dap (see Dapping: Chapter 21).

But chub may also be caught in more open water by
fishing exactly as you would fish for trout, with nymph
or wet fly or dry fly. In either case, it is advisable, I
think, to use a fairly hefty fly. The chub likes a good
mouthful. I don't say that he will refuse a small fly,
but he has a very big mouth, and when he opens it he
likes to engulf something substantial. The conventional big Palmer-tied chub fly, red or black or brown,
or a big 'variant' spider, or a Zulu, will usually do the
trick. But a big wet March Brown is a great fly at this
game, and Ivens Green Nymph—a marvellous lake fly
—has taken fish, to my certain knowledge. So has a
Hardy shrimp.

If the chub are lying across river from your stance,
and you can reach them comfortably, a flasher such as
the Butcher or silver-bodied March Brown or Alexandra—any 'minnow fly', in fact—will take fish if you
can arrange to bring it round past the chub's nose. In
fact, if you can cast right into the far bank and then
hang on, so that the fly, pulled by the current working
on the line, suddenly skids round and changes direction right in front of the fish's nose, you will get a pull,
with any luck.

In autumn, when the fish are not so fond of lying

just under the surface, I usually fish in the conventional cross-and-downstream fashion, with a big flasher, searching likely spots.

Dace take a fly freely and are great fun to fish for. They take and eject the fly with great rapidity, and you have to be really smart on the strike. In bright weather you will find the dace lying all over the river, but particularly in fast glides.

Dry-fly fishing for dace, exactly as you would angle for trout lying on the fin and ready to take surface flies, can give fast and furious sport. Dace are relatively unlikely to take alarm at a splashy cast, and you can take fish after fish from a shoal without unduly alarming the others. Any *small* fly, within reason, will attract them—remember that they are small fish with very small mouths. A tiny hackle fly (size ooo, new style, or No. 18, old style) tied on to a 4X or 5X leader is the medicine: a Wickham, a Greenwell's Glory, a Black Gnat, or an Olive of one shade or another.

Dace will also take the wet fly or nymph, again provided that it is small. But they take—and eject—so speedily that there is really very little chance of getting them on a sunken *line*. It is upstream greased-line fishing all the time, and the fly must either be floating or barely sunken (say six inches to a foot) if you are to give yourself half a chance of hooking them.

After a day with the dace your timing for trout fishing will be ruined. You will have to get back into the habit of the slow, deliberate strike.

Roach sometimes rise and take flies from the surface, especially lake roach on calm summer evenings. Then a small Black Spider, Tup, Wickham, or Greenwell will serve, on a fine leader. They suck the fly in quite deliberately.

I have never caught a river roach on dry fly, myself, but there is no doubt at all that it has been done. But I have taken them on the true nymph, fished very deep. The trouble is that you get so little notice. There is almost no way of knowing that a fish has taken your nymph into its mouth—unless the water is perfectly clear, and your eyesight superb. It is very much a hit-and-miss affair, for me at any rate, and I fish the fly for roach only when they are rising in a lake after a hot day. Roach will not attack a flasher, that represents a small fish. They are not carnivorous—unless you call it carnivorous to eat flies and nymphs. So it is no good fishing for *them* with a Butcher thrown downstream.

Rudd are exceedingly obliging at times. Lake rudd, which hang around by reedy banks, will often take a dry or a sunken fly with abandon, and when they are 'on' you can have a fine time—provided you approach them craftily enough. It is best done from a boat, casting in towards the bank. Any fly or nymph within reason: again, no flashers. If no fish attacks your small fly within about half a minute, recover it by tiny twitches. This will often bring a fish to investigate the moving and apparently living thing. The leader must not be stouter than 4X—and a healthy, beautiful rudd will put up a great fight on such gear.

Since perch live mainly on fish and will attack almost anything that moves and looks vaguely fishy, it is not surprising that they are the spinner's best friend. But by the same token, they will also take a fly. They will take a true fly—a nymph, I should say, for they rarely if ever rise to the surface—but they will also, and more eagerly, take a flasher. I have had perch from lakes and river, fishing a Butcher or an Alexandra *very fast*. I use a big fly, for the perch is another who likes a big mouthful. And he has a big mouth. However, you must be fairly careful when handling a hooked perch, for that big mouth is very soft and fleshy, and the hook-hold may give if you are hamfisted. Fly fishing for perch is essentially sunken-line fishing, just as fly fishing for dace is essentially a greased-line business.

Pike, I may say without much fear of contradiction, are rarely angled for of set purpose with the fly. It seems rather a pity, for there is no doubt that pike have been caught on the fly, even though accidentally, and they have the aggressive characteristics which make them potential fly-takers. I am always promising myself that I will have a real go for pike with a big, flashy fly, perhaps a salmon fly or a Terror: I never set about it. But I have little doubt that if you could make a flashy fly turn and skid away in front of a pike's nose, as described in the section on chub fishing, you would stand a fair chance, or better than fair, of stimulating that fish into action. Of course, you would have to locate your fish quite precisely, for pike are not in the habit of moving far in search of food if they can help it—unlike the roving perch—and your chances are much higher if you bring the meal to the pike.

Pike or no, you see that there is ample scope for the fly fisher in pursuit of the so-called 'coarse' fish. The real beauty of it is that the fly will take fish on those summer days when baits seem absolutely useless. And that great experimentalist, my pal Fred J. Taylor, has recently shown us all that you can indeed take pike by fly fishing—not many, true, but what fun!

CHAPTER 21

Dapping

Dapping is a time-honoured method of fly fishing, but it is doubtful if the average fly fisher would call it fly fishing at all. Yet it *is*, and on its day it can be most productive. You should at least know about it. One day, however superior you may feel, you will use it, and thereby save a blank.

In fact, dapping is undoubtedly the original method of fly fishing. It is restricted in its scope, and has been, so to speak, superseded by fly casting as we know it now, which gives the fly fishermen much greater range and opportunity. Yet the utterly simple, primitive business of dapping is really the purest form of fly fishing, and, on its day and in the right circumstances, will take fish surely.

Dapping consists of letting a fly down on to the surface of the water. That is all there is to it. Instead of casting the fly, you simply lower it on to the surface. That is the distinction between dapping and fly casting.

You do not need a fly rod and fly line to indulge in dapping.

Dapping divides into two separate and distinct branches. There is long-range or 'horizontal' dapping with the aid of the wind, and there is short-range or 'vertical' dapping with the aid of gravity.

Dapping further subdivides into dapping with the natural insect and dapping with the artificial.

Long-range or horizontal dapping with the aid of the wind is a method still much used, especially in Ireland, or Eire, in the Mayfly season. You use a very long, light rod—fifteen feet is not too long. 'Dapping rods' are made, and doubtless sold; but you can

manage very well with an ordinary light roach rod—
provided it has a top part strong enough to handle a
big trout! There is also such a thing as a special dapping line, traditionally a line of light 'floss silk'. But
modern thin monofilament nylon, as used by the
habitual roach fisher, will in fact serve, though not so
well. The point is that the line must be carried out by
the wind. The angler does no casting.

There you are, sitting in your boat, with a fair
breeze blowing, and fish tending to rise to the surface
to take the hatching fly. You have your back to the
wind and the point of your rod going out in the direction in which the wind is blowing. You have a fly on
the end of your cast. You pull the floss silk line off your
ordinary centre-pin reel, and the wind catches it and
draws it out over the water. You get out as much line
as the wind will carry, and then you start to fish by
letting the fly down until it touches the water. By
manipulating the rod (you see why it is advantageous
to have a long rod) and by taking advantage of the
vagaries of the breeze, you make the fly dance on the
ripples, sometimes resting quietly for a few moments,
sometimes fluttering on and off the surface like a
hatching insect. Sooner or later a large neb will break
the surface and a large trout (we hope) will suck in
your fly. Your boatman helps you by manoeuvring the
boat to take fullest advantage of the breeze, and so you
drift quietly, covering a lot of water without the
slightest muscular exertion on your part.

It is a lazy and very productive way of fishing still
water from a boat, and I have also seen it done from
the shore, given the right sort of wind. As I said, it is
customarily practised in the Mayfly season, especially
on Irish loughs where the trout do not normally rise to
surface flies except at Mayfly time.

I know of no reason why this method should not be
used habitually on lakes anywhere, at any time—given
the breeze to do the work. I admit I have not put this
theory into practice, but, like so many fly fishers, I

actually enjoy the work of casting so much that I am not often feeling lazy enough to want to dap. When I feel that lazy, I fish for carp, sitting on a groundsheet. But dapping is actually far more efficient than casting, when you have the wind to work it. The best of casters cannot help his heavy line coming down on the water. It is far more likely that a fish will confidently take a fly which just comes down and kisses the water, with, apparently, no strings to it. However, we are creatures of convention.

Whether to use a natural or an artificial insect is a problem on which no one should be dogmatic. No doubt the natural insect is more attractive, but its inherent attractiveness is offset by the difficulty of keeping it alive on a hook—not to mention the difficulty of obtaining it! Neatly and lightly hooked between segments of the body, a large insect will keep alive and kicking for a short time, but it is always chancy. Irish anglers, or at least Irish ghillies, favour several insects bunched together. There is a very ingenious hook incorporating a spring clip which holds the insect lightly but tenaciously without injuring it at all. Otherwise, use a hook that is wide in the gape and light in the wire.

Favoured insects for this form of fly fishing are, first, the Mayfly in its season, then, the grasshopper—a really killing lure—the sedges, the bluebottle, the humble bee, and the daddy-long-legs or crane fly.

The other form of dapping—vertical or gravity-powered—is entirely different in execution, though basically it obeys the same laws. It is used when fish are lying close up under a river-bank, underneath tangled vegetation, bushes, or overhanging trees, which make a normal *cast* impossible.

In such a situation, if you know or suspect that there is a fish lurking there waiting for insects to fall from the brush, you pinch a split-shot on to your leader about six inches above your fly. You then wind the leader round and round your rod tip until only a few inches are hanging down.

Moving with an Indian's stealth, you work your way into a position from which you can insinuate the rod top through the brush directly over the fish's lie. You then craftily unwind the leader by turning the rod round and round. The weight of the split-shot takes it down, and you let it alight on the surface of the water slightly upstream—you hope—of the fish's nose. You can let it drift a foot or so, or you can make it dap or dib it up and down, on and off the surface.

This is a breathlessly exciting, tense business. You usually see everything that happens, though yourself unseen. You see the fish swim up, open his mouth, engulf your fly, and turn down again.

What you do when you have hooked the fish is strictly your problem. No one can help you—least of all a writer. In the circumstance envisaged, it is a real problem to land the fish after rising him. Some habitual shrub-creepers use stout gut—it doesn't matter, since it is never seen on the water—and stout rod tops, even so stout as a pike rod. You have to decide for yourself how much you want the fish and how much, or how little, you enjoy this stealthy game of stalking a given fish and persuading it to take your dapped fly. I may say that very fine big fish frequently lie in such places, where an orthodox cast fly will never reach them. It is great fun if you don't mind getting scratched and if you are prepared for a real battle when you hook your fish.

I have done this sort of thing often enough, to take big chub—the sort of chub which lie in a regular thicket of obstructions—using a short salmon spinning rod and a fuzzy Palmer-tied fly, or a grasshopper.

The situation which I have described represents the very worst, most daunting circumstances. Frequently you will find it possible to take fish by dapping an ordinary fly, with an ordinary fly rod, while you hide yourself behind a tree or bush.

I should say that, so far as rivers go, dapping is the chub fisher's friend. But it is not to be despised as a means of hooking trout in difficult positions.

You may, of course, use a weighted nymph, instead of the customary floater, and let it sink to the bottom. Then you make it rise and fall by the deadly old method of 'sink and draw', beloved of the drop-minnow enthusiast and the pike hunter.

I agree, you might just as well use a worm or maggot. But it's a lot of fun, and it *is* undeniably a branch of fly fishing.

CHAPTER 22

Fly-cum-float

You think of the float fisher, no doubt, as a man who habitually fishes a *bait* on the bottom, or somewhere between the bottom and mid-water. But the float fisher may also fish the fly—with precisely the same tackle. Indeed, I know several habitual float fishers who vary their methods to suit the circumstances—always a sign of wisdom—and who are just as likely to tie on a dry fly as to put on a worm. I have done it myself often enough.

Then there was the late, great Alexander Wanless, the foremost, and most prolific, advocate of the fixed-spool reel. He made many enemies, especially among habitual fly fishers, but there is little doubt in my mind that Wanless as a publicist achieved, single-handed or very nearly so, the most far-reaching revolution in British angling since the introduction of the winch. Wanless could fish the fly on the heavy line as well as most, but he was fascinated by the technique of fishing the fly from a fixed-spool reel, with a very light line and a float. True, he tended to call the float the 'controller'—quite accurately, for in fly-cum-float fishing that is what it is.

Briefly, float-cum-fly fishing consists of casting out a fairly heavy float—preferably a plastic 'bubble' float partly filled with water—with the fly or flies some feet distant from it. Small wooden, cork, or quill floats are also used, but the almost invisible bubble float has much to commend it, in respect of inconspicuousness, though it *does* tend to make rather a splash and to create a distinct 'wake'.

You can have the float two yards or more up your leader, and the fly or flies tied on the business end, farthest away from the rod. Or you can tie the float on the very end, and have the fly or flies tied on droppers between float and rod.

The main purpose of the float, or controller, is to give you weight for casting. Once you have made your cast you fish as usual, watching the fly.

There is no doubt that this method is very useful to the man who does not wish to invest in a new outfit just for occasional fly fishing, but wishes to extend his activities sometimes when ordinary bait fishing is proving unproductive—as it often does, especially in high summer, when fish are showing more interest in the upper part of the water, and in insects.

Perhaps the most pronounced utility of this method becomes apparent when you want to drift a fly down to fish feeding at some distance below you. In such circumstances you tie the fly—nymph or floater—on the extreme end of the leader, and place the float about two yards away, nearer to the rod tip. You then cast out into the stream and let the whole works drift down on the surface, checking the float whenever it shows a tendency to overhaul the fly. In this way you present the fly to the fish without advertising that there is anything attached to it. It is, in fact, a much modified form of the 'long trotting' beloved of coarse anglers, especially on such swift but smooth gin-clear rivers as the Hampshire Avon.

It is exceedingly effective, but you can also fish a dry fly upstream, provided you have the assistance of a very light wind behind you to straighten out the cast. Dry fly, nymph, and ordinary wet flies can be fished effectively with little or no effort, certainly not a tenth of the actual physical effort involved in casting a fly with a normal fly rod and line. If the breeze is not blowing in the direction it ought, you can make your cast straighten out by checking the float as it hits the water, or just before. This will jerk it back towards you and straighten out the cast satisfactorily.

Some anglers use two and even three flies on a cast

when float fishing in this way, mixing them in the sensible ratio of one dry, one sunk, and one awash. There is little doubt, I think, that very many more trout are caught on flies which are awash than is generally realised. A truly floating fly, one that stands up well above the surface, merely resting on the surface skin of the water on the points of the hackle, represents a fully hatched dun about to take flight. But although fish do, of course, rise to such flies, they also rise freely to nymphs which are actually in the act of hatching—a difficult and dangerous process for the nymphs, in which they struggle and make a minute disturbance which must surely attract the attention of alert fish. This is why I do not worry unduly if my supposed 'dry' fly begins to get a shade waterlogged. And that is one more reason why I personally much prefer a soft-actioned so-called 'wet-fly' rod, even for dry-fly fishing. There is no need to keep false casting to get the fly utterly dry. It is, sometimes, a waste of time.

Needless to say, such fishing will not often be done with a genuine fly rod. It is, for some, a makeshift; for others, a deliberate technique used in preference to ordinary heavy-line fly fishing. In either case, the rod should be longish, stiffish, and light. The match fisher's twelve-foot or thirteen-foot glass-fibre rod is quite satisfactory, but a special rod made for the job, such as the old ten-foot-long 'Wanless' rod made by Hardy's, is the ideal. Hardy's 'Perfection' roach rod, eleven feet long, and the Fred J. Taylor 'Trotting' rod, made by Hardy's in glass fibre, will answer nicely. A fixed-spool reel loaded right up to the lip of the spool with fine nylon monofilament—about three, four, or at most five pounds breaking strain—is a *must*. I personally, when using this method, follow Wanless's tip and tie a fine gut leader to the nylon casting line, since gut sinks readily and nylon, generally speaking, being far less absorbent, does not.

The float gives you an accurate indication of where

your fly or flies is/are working, and a high degree of control over them. It is a very scientific method of fishing the sunk fly upstream, for by winding the reel handle to keep pace with the current you can keep in touch with your flies perfectly.

CHAPTER 23

Sea Trout

Sea trout, like salmon, are spawned in the shallows in fresh water, spend some time there, and then go to sea, where they grow large and strong. They return to their birthplace to spawn, and it is then that the angler gets a crack at them. Some hold that they are the most exciting fish in the world to angle for. They are game, strong, fast and tenacious, fight like furies, spend a great deal of time leaping in the air, and are delicious to eat.

No wonder that some fishermen prefer sea-trout fishing to all other forms. But there is a drawback. In rivers, at any rate in fairly small, fairly shallow, and fairly clear rivers, sea trout behave with such a high degree of shyness and circumspection that it is virtually impossible to catch them in numbers during daylight, and night fishing is then *de rigeur*. This is itself an added attraction, to some adventurous spirits; others, less enamoured of making life difficult, find that it puts them off. It is strictly a question of taste and temperament.

Luckily, for those who dislike night fishing, there are two circumstances which mitigate the severity of this pursuit. In rivers with some colour, sea trout may be taken during daylight. In lochs, they may always be taken during daylight. So if you find night fishing unduly difficult or for any reason unattractive (as I do, I admit it), then you must seek them in lochs or when the river is high and coloured by flood water.

The sea trout is also known as sewin (in Wales), as peal (in the West Country), as white trout (in Ireland), and as salmon-trout (at the fishmonger's).

Sea trout run to tremendous weights. The usual run

of 'school' fish—maiden fish returning to spawn for the
first time—may go from half a pound to nearly two
pounds, but individuals in plenty run up to something
very near ten pounds, and, exceptionally, much larger.
The British rod-caught record, taken in the Dorset-
shire Frome in 1946, weighed more than twenty-two
pounds. The big fish tend to run early and singly, the
school fish in great numbers from about June to
August. The dates vary from river to river.

It is possible to fish for sea trout, in daylight, even
when the water is clear, with the upstream dry fly. For
this purpose you need great stealth and determination,
a strong rod and sound leader, excellent eyesight, and a
strong right arm. It is very tiring work. It does not
really differ appreciably from dry-fly fishing for trout,
except inasmuch as you usually find yourself casting to
likely places rather than to rising fish.

A commoner method is the old traditional downstream wet-fly fishing—more often with a flasher or
attractor fly than with a genuine nymph, of course. For
this purpose you really need a much stouter rod than
you would use for trout fishing. Not only because the
fish run bigger, stronger, and more violent than brown
trout but also because you will be throwing a fly
appreciably bigger and heavier, *and* because in this
sport you simply must keep out of sight of the fish—
and that involves throwing a long line, pretty well as
long as you can manage, and, within reason, the longer
the better. Sea trout are extraordinarily shy and suspicious, and if they get wind of you, or of your rod, they
will assuredly ignore your flies and go right down.

I have fished for sea trout happily enough with a
nine-foot double-built rod, but mainly in troubled
water and bad light. For all-round daytime downstream fishing I would recommend a double-handed
rod of twelve or even thirteen feet, a light salmon rod.
You are casting a very long line all the time, and there
is no question but that a double-handed rod is a great
deal less tiring to use than a strong single-handed one.

Nevertheless, the rod must not be stiff and pole-like, or you will, on the one hand, lose a great deal of sport and, on the other, break in many fish. A light rod of the kind sold for greased-line salmon fishing—of which more later—is about right. A twelve-foot rod in hollow fibre-glass is ideal, especially for fishing the brackish water of estuaries, for it is unaffected by salt-water corrosion.

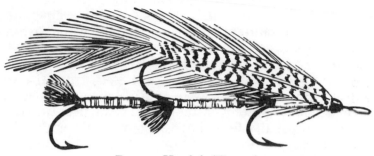

FIG. 44. Hardy's 'Terror'.

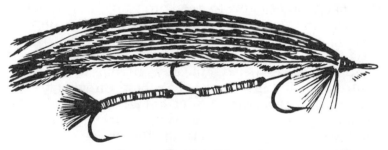

FIG. 45. Hardy's 'Demon'.

Whatever rod you choose, you have to cast so that the fly or flies—I generally use but two on the leader, and often just one—are operating well downstream of where you stand. There is no need, in my experience, to work the flies; just let them swing round in the current and retrieve a little, as in trout fishing.

Recommended good wet flies are legion; again, it is as well to get local opinion on this thorny subject. I am very doubtful if one is so much better than another. That very fine sea-trout angler, Mr. H. P. Henzell, in his definitive work *Fishing For Sea Trout* (A. & C. Black), says that he is content with two—the Butcher and the Mallard-and-Claret. Other fine flies are the teal-wing series—Teal-and-Red, Teal-and-Green, Teal-and-Silver—the Black Pennell, the good old Silver Invicta and Alexandra, the Peter Ross, and the smaller salmon flies such as the Jock Scott. I myself favour the Demons and Terrors—bright, even gaudy lures tied on tandem hooks; especially when fishing near the sea or actually *in* it.

It is often very profitable to fish actual sea pools, where you may well find sea trout fresh from the sea and more likely to take with a rush than stale fish that have become 'potted' after long residence in fresh water. You usually find that you have to draw the line fast to give vivid life to the lure.

It cannot be too strongly emphasised that when you are fishing in daylight, or even at dusk, you must take the very greatest pains to keep out of sight of sea trout. Not only is their vision fantastically good but they are also highly sensitive to vibrations. You have to step carefully and quietly and take advantage of every scrap of cover—*never*, in any circumstances, show yourself on a high bank. The best thing is to slip silently into the water under a high bank and, after working yourself into a casting position, stand perfectly still until you are certain the fish have not been frightened. Panic spreads through a school of sea trout faster than through a school of stock jobbers.

If you fancy night fishing in a river, use one fly only, a stout leader (no finer than five pounds), and learn in daytime just what it *feels* like to cast the right length of line—i.e. a length which will drop your fly into the water just short of the far bank. You have to go by the feel, since everything seems much nearer than it really is, in night fishing—so get used to the feel of the right-length cast in daytime. Disengaging your fly from

bushes at night is no joke, apart from the fact that the
commotion it causes will effectually finish your fishing
for that night! In that pool, anyway.

Some anglers impale a maggot on the fly hook when
fishing at night. I think you might as well stick to
plain bottom fishing and give up the pretence of fly
fishing altogether. Not that I am any sort of purist, but
why deceive *yourself*? Maggot fishing is maggot fishing, not fly fishing. Mark you, a fly tried with a scrap of
washleather at the butt is often good. I don't know if
the fish take it for a maggot; but it probably catches
their eye.

However, don't think that because it is dark the fish
need something particularly eye-catching. On the con-
trary. They can find a black fly on a black night with
astounding ease. The trouble is hooking them. Sometimes you will find a sea trout taking with a rush and a
bang. More often not. The late Lindsay Gray, a great
West Country angler for salmon and sea trout, told me
that in his opinion fish which *do* take with a bang are
fish which have had to dash out on seeing the fly pass
their lie, seize it and turn back to the lie. Normally,
fish which are lying out in the stream take a fly very
gently indeed: all you feel is the gentlest of plucks.
Unless your strike is instantaneous you will land nothing.

Once a sea trout *is* hooked, watch out! Nothing in
the world of fishes moves so fast and so furiously. Bass
and carp are relatively as strong and perhaps as fast,
on occasion—but the sea trout's peculiarity is his fond-
ness for leaping in the air and suddenly doubling back
on his course, coming right for you like an express
train. Sometimes he will shake the hook out when he
leaps. Sometimes he will come down again before you
have dipped your rod point, and the resulting sudden
tightening-up will break the leader. Sometimes the hook
will fall out when he does his fabulous about-turn act
and races towards you far faster than you can reel in.
Either way, you have your hands full. *Never* try to net

a sea trout, even a small one, until he is played right out and on his side. And even when he is in the net, never pick him out unless you are sure you have a really effective grip—which means a finger under the gill plates.

Fishing for sea trout in lakes and lochs, from a boat, is not very dissimilar to lake fishing for brownies. A light rod for wet fly—mine is a nine-footer weighing a shade more than five ounces—will master the best of fish, if the water is free from snags and the angler takes control firmly at the start. If the water is snag-infested, weedy, or full of sharp rocks, a stronger rod is called for—a ten-footer, perhaps, with a correspondingly stronger leader. But you will raise more fish with light gut, and enjoy your fishing much more.

If there is a breeze to raise a beautiful concealing ripple, then wet-fly fishing is natural. You cast out into the wind and let your flies sink. You work them back to you for a short distance by pulling in line with the left hand. After a time when your top or bob fly is getting to the surface, change your method of working the flies. Raise the rod top and make the bob fly bob—that is, dance upon the surface. It is very near to dapping, but you still have sunk flies working for you as well as the bobber. Fish may take near to the boat, so go on working your lures right to the end.

Early and late in the sea-trout season you may find that it pays to get the flies well down. In the middle season you may, if the weather holds warm, find them nearer the top.

The dry fly is indicated when there is a flat calm. (You can only work your wet flies successfully when there is a breeze.) True, a flat calm is terrible bad weather for lake fishing, anyway, but a dry fly will sometimes produce. Cast a good long line, well away from the boat, and *let the fly rest* for a long time—as much as ten minutes. A cruising fish may spot it. If no fish happens along in ten minutes, give your dry fly a twitch or two, wait a minute, then draw it back towards you in a series of slight, spaced twitches. Don't, however, work it right back to the boat. Pick it off the water neatly when it is still some distance away, and try another sector. And if unsuccess persists, try another fly. It is dicey work at best, but well worth trying in a calm—better than not fishing at all.

Cruising across the mouth of an estuary in a boat you can often spot sea trout moving in—especially if there is weed about. They often investigate weed. You can track their course in the open sea, and a Demon or Terror cast across in front of the fish and moved briskly through the water, in jerks, will often take one.

Sea trout are thought of as *habitués* of the fast, steep rivers of Wales, the West Country, and Scotland. True enough. But there *is* a distinct run of large sea trout in such unlikely and relatively sluggish waters as the Sussex Ouse, Arun, and Rother. They are more often taken by spinning, or on the worm. But the fly fisher stuck in those parts might care to have a go at putting a feathered lure over the water. I sometimes do.

CHAPTER 24

Salmon: Fly or Spinner?

No doubt about it, the king of fish. 'God made salmon just the right size,' said one philosopher whose name eludes me now that I need it. And, indeed, it is so: neither so huge that you have to fish for him with poles and ropes (I can never bring myself to heavy sea fishing, the so-called 'big game' fishing) nor so small that he seems insignificant in those occasional moments of depression when you wonder, really, if angling is worthwhile. (Oh yes, we all have them.) Just right is the salmon. You can take him on tackle light enough to be responsible and alive in the hand, yet he is big enough to thrill the most blasé.

Unfortunately, salmon costs money, and therefore salmon fishing is expensive, too. In his book *Torridge Fishery*, L. R. N. Gray records that salmon-fishing rights were worth £10 000 per mile per bank way back in 1957. You can hardly expect to get good salmon fishing cheap. However, since every fish you catch is worth an average of £1 a pound, you can get some of your expenses back if you take the trouble to learn to fish well.

Even more unfortunately, spinning is steadily—no, not steadily: *rapidly*—ousting fly fishing as a popular means of fishing for salmon. I enjoy spinning very much, but I am in no two minds about the relative pleasures of heaving out a spinning lure and casting a fly. I think *most* anglers would come to agree, if they gave both a trial, that fly fishing is more fun.

But, even so, many are scared off fly fishing because they believe that spinning is much more productive and more likely to get them fish—i.e. fivers. Now I doubt if this is really so. Probably more fish are caught

on the spinner than on the fly—but only because more
anglers use the spinning rod than use the fly rod. I
would not care to put myself forward as any sort of
authority on salmon fishing—I can afford only the
snatched, short holiday, rarely indeed on really superb
water—but I think a majority of really expert salmon
men would confirm that the fly, properly fished, will
actually beat the spinner. I am sure of it myself, and
far better men tell me that *is* so.

I suppose there is some sort of notion current that fly
fishing is more difficult than spinning. Untrue! It is
easier. But I think we should add this rider: indifferent fly fishing will land fewer fish than indifferent
spinning, but good fly fishing will land more fish than
good spinning. It is a case of competence really paying
off.

I am not very competent myself, if only because I
have not had a great deal of experience. Again, a question of means and opportunity. But I have done
enough, and fished under the tutelage of enough really
good salmon fishers, to know the difference between
mediocre and good salmon fishing. This knowledge I
will now pass on to you, and you can rely on it, for it
comes from first-rate salmon fishers.

CHAPTER 25

Salmon: The Life Story

First—because without it we can only grope in the dark, not knowing what we are doing or why—a potted biography of King Salmon.

The salmon comes to life in the headwaters of a river, on a shallow, gravelly 'redd'. Hatched out from the egg, it lives precariously for several years—at least two, possibly three, more often two. The salmon grows to about six inches long in fresh water, and is known as a parr. It looks all too like a small trout at this stage. It feeds and lives exactly like a trout, competing for the same food. It takes the sunken fly ravenously, and is often destroyed by ignorant men who think they have a trout.

Then the young salmon—now called a smolt—slips down to the sea. Obeying an ancestral call which it cannot ignore, it runs straight out to the deeps. Just where it goes, nobody in the wide world really knows for sure. It goes a long way—probably halfway round the world. It feeds enormously—on what? Nobody is sure: possibly herrings, prawns, elvers—and it grows at a great pace. One year later, sometimes two, it returns to the river of its birth.

It is now sexually mature. The urge which sends it back is the paternal, maternal urge: the invincible biological urge to perpetuate the species. For this, it abandons its rich feeding in the depths. It enters the cold, thin water of its parent river. Reluctantly, we must assume, exchanging abundance and the semi-security of the ample depths for the meagre cover, the starvation, of the fresh-water river.

Back in the river, the salmon fasts. That is to say, it ceases to feed purposefully. It snaps at things now and

again—if it didn't, no salmon fisher would ever catch a
fish—but it digests little or nothing. Its digestive
organs have begun to atrophy from disuse before ever
it enters the river. It takes food, not often, out of habit,
or merely because, when oxygen is abundant and the
temperature right, it feels good. Nobody knows *for
sure* just why it takes a fly or bait. Oftener than not, it
doesn't.

Rivers vary, but, by and large, the run of salmon
begins while it is still winter, with relatively few big
fish forcing their way up on flood water. Later in the
year the summer fish run, and as a rule they are
smaller—maiden fish returning for the first time,
known as 'grilse', as small as four pounds, as big as ten
to twelve pounds.

Salmon will not run up-river unless there is adequate flow of water coming down. They run freely in
high water; in low water they skulk in the deeps and
move only by night, if at all.

A fish that is travelling is a likely taker. A fish that
has been 'potted' too long in one pool is dour and
sulky. The taking fish is usually one that has just
moved up into a new pool and has only begun to settle
down there. The rate at which salmon travel up-river
is debated. Sometimes they drop down before going up
again.

Eventually the salmon reach the spawning grounds,
high up near the source of the river. It is autumn.
Some spawning fish may have been in the river for
months. Some, lucky in their ample travelling water,
may be almost fresh from the sea. The longer a fish
stays in the river, literally living off its fat, and growing uneasy, the less palatable its flesh becomes. It becomes 'red': it loses its silvery sea coat. It can actually
become sun-burned. Salmon hate the bright sunlight.

The hen fish scoops out a depression in the gravel
and lays her eggs. The male or cock fish, hovering near,
deposits its milt or sperm on the eggs, fertilising them.
Then they descend again to the sea. Very few reach

it. Now they are called kelts—spent fish, thin, tasteless, flabby, and protected by law. No kelt may be gaffed or kept. Gaffs are illegal early in the season, when the river is usually full of kelts: a humane tailer must be used, which enables you to return the fish unharmed if it proves to be a kelt.

Few cock fish get back to the sea. The majority die. Many hen fish die, too, but some reach the sea, to wax fat and mighty again. They return to the river—two, three, even four times, growing ever mightier (and coarser in the flesh).

That is the life-cycle of the salmon, in rough and in miniature.

CHAPTER 26

Salmon and the Sunken Fly

Fly fishing for salmon is divided strictly into two modes, sunken fly and greased-line. You must know *why*.

Early in the season, when the water is cold, salmon which enter the river hug the bottom. To attract them you must fish your fly or bait right near the bottom of the river. They are relatively torpid and will not travel far to seize your lure. It must be a big lure—near enough three inches long.

Your line, then, must be heavy, to sink well. Your fly, too, must be heavy—or at least large. What does it represent? Heaven knows. Certainly *not* an insect, though it is called a fly. It is made of traditional fly-tying materials—that is to say, fur and feather and tinsel and so on—but it represents nothing that ever flew.

Perhaps it represents a small fish. Very likely. Or a prawn or shrimp. Possible. Or—as that genius among salmon fishers, Mr. Richard Waddington, has strongly suggested—it may represent a young eel, an elver. It surely represents something fishy to which the salmon is well accustomed, in the sea.

It is from two to three inches long. Enormous for a 'fly', but no bigger than the spinner's spring-time lure, the sprat or loach or Devon minnow.

Now plainly, to present this lump to a salmon lying torpid in deep water—perhaps as deep as twelve feet—you have to use substantial means. A stout, strong rod. A heavy line. A stout gut leader.

The pull of the water when you recover your fly for the back cast is itself something quite tremendous—heaving up a thick line out of a strong current which has it grasped, deep down, imposes a terrific strain on the rod. More of a strain in fact, than the actual business of casting the fly thirty-odd yards through the air.

Ergo, a powerful rod. Twelve feet is becoming quite a fashionable length, but it is far too short, I believe. Far from making your work lighter, it makes it greatly heavier. The trend for short, light rods has gone too far. Work it out: a short, stiff rod makes *you* do the work of putting a flex into it. A longer, gentler-actioned rod does most of the work for you. By saving an ounce or two in weight you may well be putting an intolerable strain on your muscles.

For sunk-line fishing, then, a powerful but flexible rod of not less than thirteen feet in length. There has been a great vogue since the Second World War for the spliced greenheart rod. Grant 'Vibration' rods have had a terrific vogue, mainly because one or two angling writers laid it down that they were the *only* tools which would switch or Spey cast (of which, more later). It is simply not true. A perfectly made built-cane rod will Spey cast as well as a spliced greenheart and come out many ounces lighter. An Apollo tubular-steel rod, the thirteen-foot 'Clytha' or the fifteen-foot 'Moy', is perfect for the job, if you can find one. Of course, good greenheart *is* good, and good spliced greenheart is beautiful to use. But it is far heavier, less reliable, less powerful than cane or tubular steel. And more difficult to come by. Good glass salmon rods are now available in all lengths at reasonable prices.

Whatever rod you choose, it must be strong enough to throw an A.F.T.M. 9 or even 10 line. This is the lightest line that will sink far enough and fast enough to get your fly down to bottom-hugging spring salmon. A tapered line is a luxury, not necessary at all unless you have to do the Spey cast. A level line will do very well indeed, for ordinary overhead casting: a novice will find it actually helpful, and *much* cheaper. But if the bank of the river you fish is heavily tree'd or bush'd, and you therefore have to use the trick casts—

Spey, switch, or steeple—then a tapered line is essential. A forward-taper or torpedo-head line is useless for Spey casting, delightful for overhead casting—but not a bit nice to fish with.

FIG. 46. Telescopic Gaff.
(*Courtesy Ogden Smith's.*)

A good big plain reel, reliable and capable of holding the line, plus *at least* eighty yards of braided silk or braided nylon backing spliced to it, completes the machinery. You will also need a tailer to pick the beaten fish out of the water—or a gaff, if you are fishing somewhat later in the season when kelts do not

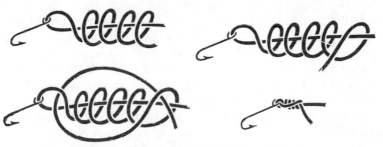

FIG. 47. The Trapped Half-blood Knot.

have to be considered. I always prefer the tailer. It does not disfigure the fish.

For early fishing, you need not worry about fine leaders. In fact, to carry that huge fly, and to deal with big fish in heavy water, your leader *must* be stout, new, and true. Make a real job of tying the fly on—I give a useful knot, the trapped half-blood. You can't beat it.

Now fishing the big sunk fly is simplicity itself, once you have mastered the two basic rules: *slow* and *deep*. Deep and slow. No spring salmon, appalled to find himself thrust by obscure instinct into the thin water

and the unwontedly restricted area of a river, is going
to dash across the stream to chase your fly. It must
come across his very nose, or near enough, and it must
come slowly.

Now see for yourself. Your spring river is full and
swift. If you cast your fly more or less directly across
the stream, as you may well do when fishing the
sunken fly downstream for trout, the powerful current
will immediately seize the belly of the line and snatch
it downstream. The fly, pulled willy-nilly by the moving line, dashes across the stream at a tremendous
pace. No salmon is going to race after it. Bucking the
current at high speed, it is behaving as no tiny fish
could behave. No salmon is going to be deceived by
that.

The answer, then, is to cast as long a line as you can
and to cast it almost directly downstream, at a very
narrow angle to the current. The longer the line
(trigonometry specialists note), the longer the time it
will take the fly to travel across the short arc which the
end of the line describes as it swings across the river.

However, that is only the elementary start of sunk-
fly fishing. The thing you really have to concentrate on
is *the belly of the line*. Remember, it is the pressure of
the current on the belly of the line which determines
the speed at which your fly travels across-current. Now
in fast water, aim *not* to have a curved belly in your
line. Keep it straight. In slacker water, aim to *put* a
curved belly in the line, so that the current, working
on this, will speed up your fly. For your fly will not
bear very close inspection in slack water. If the salmon
sees too much of it, it may decide that there is something awfully fishy—or, rather, *un*fish-like—in this
weird creation. And leave it severely alone.

Repeat. If the place you are fishing is slower, quieter
water, you put a belly in your line, and the belly leads
the fly across. You do this simply. The moment your fly
hits the water, you lift the point of the rod quite
vigorously and toss a portion of line over to one side,

either your left or your right according to which side
you are standing. And *lead* the line over by keeping
your point over to one side. But if the water is very
fast, cast almost directly downstream, as straight a line
as you can, and do no leading with the rod. Gradually
the current will move the line over until it is, indeed,
perfectly straight downstream, along the centre-line of
the prevailing current. If the current is *too* fast, slow
the fly down by putting an *upstream* belly into the
line. It is the fly's speed *across* the current that counts.
Small fish swim slowly, feebly.

How to cast? With a double-handed rod it is simplicity itself—*far,* far easier than with a single-handed
trout rod. The only thing you have to remember is NOT
TO WAGGLE THE ROD BUTT BACKWARDS AND FORWARDS IN
YOUR HANDS. No 'see-saw' movement. The left hand—I
am assuming that you are a right-handed angler—the
left hand holds the button quite lightly *and does not
move either backwards or forwards*. The button is, in
fact, cupped in the palm of the left hand. *This point is
the fulcrum.* Casting is *not* a matter of pushing one
hand out and pulling the other hand in. It is easy to
fall into this error; easy, and fatal to really long casting. You make an ordinary overhead cast thus:

You have fished out a cast. The line is lying straight
downstream from you. The butt is horizontal, extended out over the water, a continuation of the line,
more or less in the same plane. To make the back cast,
lift the entire rod, smartly. Your left hand, cupping
the button, rises more or less to the level of your chin.
While you do this, holding the button so that it does
not move either forwards or backwards, but simply
rises in a vertical plane, pull back hard with the right
hand.

Thus you put a severe bend into the rod—your
muscular effort, plus the weight of the extended line,
plus the pull of the water. These three factors put a
forward bend into the rod. Immediately it recovers,
reacting powerfully against this stress. It straightens

and, in fact, goes backwards—the top portion only—
carrying the line with it, to stream out overhead and
behind, exactly as in single-handed casting. You help
this reaction by pulling back strongly with your right
hand.

When the line is almost fully extended behind, but
not quite, you give it the forward impulse—again the
right hand making the movement—and the line goes
over forwards and falls on the water. As it hits the
water, you lower the left hand, cupping the button,
allow the rod to sink to a horizontal plane, and you
are fishing.

That is the simple mechanics of the plain overhead
cast. Never waggle the rod between the hands. It can
stand repeating. Lift *the entire rod* to give the line a
good start up off the water—which exerts a great pull
on it. Use the whole body, *not* simply the arms. Legs,
shoulders, and back all play their part.

The back cast, again, is the all-important one. You
really must snatch that line *up* off the water and get it
travelling. You open your shoulders and put a lot of
steam into that lift and back cast. The legs help a lot.
You really work at this one.

Then the forward cast is nothing, simply nothing.
The rod reacts violently against the bend which you
put into it on the back cast. The rod straightens itself,
and overstraightens, with vim and gusto (if it is a
strong, good rod). Your own part in the forward cast is
relatively mild, and mainly directional. There is no
need to flog the line forward and down (unless you
happen to be fishing into the teeth of an upstream gale
of wind). Just a strong, firm impulsion, and out she
flies. But never, never will you achieve a clean, good
forward cast unless you put some vim into a crisp,
snappy, snatching back cast.

There is a variation—indeed, a family of variations
—on this elementary cast, and the time may well come
when you will need to know them. If trees behind you,
or a high bank, or bushes, or any other obstruction,

prevent you from making the overhead cast, then you have to resort to that delightful bag of tricks known variously as the Spey or switch cast, or perhaps the steeple. They are easy to do—but, unfortunately, they are terribly hard to describe in words, and even harder to draw or to photograph. Here goes for a try.

The *steeple* cast is nothing difficult. It simply means that instead of throwing the line behind you, you throw it straight up into the air. When it is at its nearest to vertical, you flick it forward. Nothing to it. It is not a nice cast at all: it leads to some heavy splashing and occasionally, if not oftener, you find yourself with the line wrapped several times round your neck and the fly embedded in your ear. Nasty.

The switch or Spey cast is another kettle of fish—not easy to pick up, but easy once you have the knack: always rather strenuous, and, properly done, rather beautiful. And immensely useful on a wooded river. Try hard. (*I* shall have to.)

Once again, let's imagine that the line is lying directly downstream of you. You have fished out a cast. You take a pace or two downstream and the line goes out as you move. Now you are ready to cast again. The action is almost continuous and uninterrupted; fluent and smooth and almost all in one. But for the sake of clarity, I must treat it as if it were made in three separate moves. There *are* three separate phases of this cast, but they must flow one into the other. Never forget that.

Phase One. Arms fully extended, lift the whole rod, picking up as much line off the water as you can. Don't just raise the tip—raise the rod until your right arm is straight out from the shoulder and the rod is pointing upwards.

Phase Two. Without moving the feet, do a smart right turn, swinging the rod round through ninety degrees. This part of the movement to be done with immense vigour. The line will come racing back towards you. The belly of the line should fly behind you

—but the fly remains in the water. The fly *must* remain in the water—though only just. At the conclusion of this phase, ideally, the fly is just kissing the water level with your knees and a yard or two to your right. The belly of the line bulges out behind you.

Phase Three. Roll the line forward again vigorously. The rod point goes forward and upwards, the belly of the line is rolled forward again, and the fly naturally follows it. The fly is never far above the surface of the water—and it has never at any time gone behind you.

Important. In Phase Two, when you are doing your smart right turn, the arms are pretty rigid and the rod does not wobble in the hands. As you begin to sweep round, lower the point of the rod a little and raise it again as you come to the end of the turn. Then as you go forward, the rod tip first rises and then falls. Thus, you see, the rod tip actually describes an ellipse in the air. This is important. I left it out when describing the phases, for clarity's sake. (I hope.)

This cast and its several variants—you can work a few variations out for yourself once you have mastered the basic movement(s)—is terribly useful when you haven't room to throw the line out behind you. Never forget that the fly and a fraction of the leader should kiss the water at your side at the end of the 'back' cast (Phase Two). Then when you give the forward impulsion, the fly holds until the belly of the line is travelling forward, and then the belly picks it up and flings it forward. This way, with a really good rod, you ought to be able to roll a line out for thirty-odd yards. Aim for that. It is, of course, murder on the rod.

Incidentally, you can do exactly the same switching cast with a single-handed trout rod. Often, you *have* to.

In between each cast—any sort of cast, overhead or otherwise—you take two paces downstream. Some anglers take only one, but I think it is the consensus of expert opinion that this is a waste of fishing time. Fish can see a long way. You are wasting time if you fish over the same water again and again—and *not* improving your chances. Take at least two full paces between casts, three or four if you feel like it.

The great difficulty in sunken-line fishing for salmon is *hooking* the fish. Since your line is almost directly downstream, the tendency if you strike is to pull the fly out of the fish's mouth. So—never strike. Never. Never. NEVER.

If a fish moves out to take your fly, it will move back to the spot where it was lying when your fly lured it out. Your line will stop, *or* you will feel a tug. Or both. Whichever indication you get that a fish has taken your fly into its mouth, your course of action remains identical. It is, simply—*do nothing at all.*

I know it sounds absurd. At first you simply cannot bring yourself to it. But it is the only way. When your line stops, or when you feel a tug, drop the rod point even farther and let go the yard of line which you are holding lightly by the left hand, or trapped—*lightly*—against the butt by the forefinger of the right hand. That is to say, let the line go as free as it will. Some even pull off a yard or two of line from the reel. The current takes the belly of the line downstream, remorselessly, and the pull of the current it is which pulls the hook home. If you raise the rod and strike, you will merely pull the fly out of the salmon's mouth. Let the current do it. When you are satisfied that the line is quite stationary, then raise the rod and you will feel the fish on. *Then* give a good pull to make certain if you like. Not before.

This technique is possible only because the salmon is not quick to eject even a hard, alien object like a salmon fly. It will hold the fly in its mouth for several seconds. Indeed, some say that the salmon cannot eject a fly. I don't believe that, but the fact is that it is far slower than a trout to spit it out. From this alone comes the possibility of hooking salmon on the sunken fly.

Even so, you will miss fish. Everybody does. You miss them because the conventional big salmon fly is so deadly inefficient as a hooking instrument. The single hook of a big (8/o) salmon fly is a monstrous great thing. It *may* catch hold; more likely it will not. If it lies flat on the salmon's tongue—as it probably does, more often than not—then the pull of the line, instead of putting the point home, will simply pull the hook out of the fish's mouth.

So inefficient is the old 'meat hook' salmon fly that I

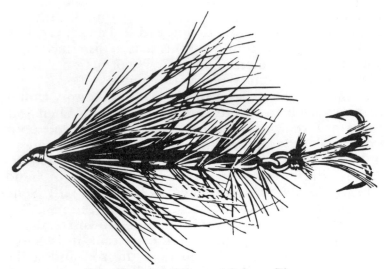

FIG. 48. A 'Waddington' Salmon Fly.

never use it. I use exclusively the newer tube flies and/ or 'Waddington' flies, both of which have small treble hooks which are infinitely more certain hookers. But if you prefer the look of the traditional salmon fly, then I recommend flies dressed on Hardy's short-point *double* hooks. These doubles are far more effective than the big single. Easier to pull in over the short barb, and far less likely to slide flat out of the fish's mouth without making penetration. Some anglers say that the fish uses a second point to lever the other out. A likely tale, I must say.

Salmon flies are peculiar creations. The old conven-

tional kind cost the earth—as much as £1 for one
fly—and they are undoubtedly works of art. They are
built up, as you see from Pézare's sketch, meticulously,
according to ancient rites, and salmon-fly dressers
would die rather than omit one solitary feature. The
proper place for these works of art is in a glass case. I
have a set framed on my study wall. They look simply
beautiful there, and they can do nobody any harm. My
wife wears one in a hat, and that is a good use for it.

To show you just how important or unimportant it
is to follow the old rules faithfully, I give here a

FIG. 49. Component parts of a conventional Salmon Fly.

picture of a 'fly' made up in a few minutes by a friend
of mine, Mr. Bill Cumper. It is a variant of the modern
tube flies—that is to say, the body consists of a hollow
tube. The tube, in this case, consists of a bit of electric
wire insulating conduit, of various colours, called Systoflex. On this the enterprising Cumper built a body
consisting of a wrapping of toffee paper, with a few
turns of hackle (brown) taken from a farmyard fowl,
and the whole secured with fuse wire (5-A). The
long fluttering tail is just a few brown hackles from a
rooster. A bit of Alasticum trace wire goes through the
tube, and a tiny treble is tied on the end. Rough, isn't
it? Fly dressers would feel insulted if they were asked
to turn out such a fly. Yet this very fly which you see
here illustrated hooked three salmon within an hour,
on the Itchen, one nasty day in the spring of 1957. I
ate a steak of the largest myself.

The vivid success of this creation led friend Bill to
do some development work—all in the direction of

even greater simplicity. All farmyard feathers and hackles were scrapped in favour of hair from a grey squirrel's tail, this material being found to behave more attractively in the water. It was also preferred on the grounds of increased durability and even easier construction. (Not to mention the fact that it provided an excuse for gunplay in the dense beechwoods on the slopes of the Downs.)

These squirrel-tail flies we tied in various sizes from

Fig. 50. The Cumper Tube Fly.

half an inch to three inches long. The small ones were armed with small double hooks, the big ones with small trebles, tied directly to the point of the cast; which was, of course, first passed through the tube. The dressings are rather bulky compared with the sleekness of some professional tyings—quite a bunch of hair tied in 'all round' at the head of the tube, using the good old 5-A fuse wire (which helps what would otherwise be a rather buoyant fly to submerge smartly). Bodies are green, red, blue, yellow, silver, and blue-and-silver. Though they are still novel enough to look strange in the hand, fished fast they have proved immensely attractive—not only to salmon but to trout and sea trout, too. Yet you can tie one in a minute, and at trifling cost.

So don't be hidebound about salmon flies.

The great Richard Waddington, I believe, began it all. He designed the Waddington fly, which is not only a great hooker but has the advantage of swimming on an even keel and of looking fish-like from whatever angle the salmon sees it: from above as well as from below. The tube fly is another development on the same general lines. Both are much cheaper than the traditional article, much less attractive to the human eye, must more efficient as hookers, and—from all I can gather—no less efficient, to put it at the lowest, in luring fish to take them.

However, you will please yourself. The old style is prettier and you may have more confidence in it. That is profoundly important.

As to dressings of fly, the basic rule is a bright fly for a bright day, a dark fly for a dark day, an in-between fly for an in-between day. When considering *tone*, remember that the colour of the river-bed enters into it. Historically speaking, the Jock Scott may well be the most successful of all salmon flies. The Ackroyd is called 'the poor man's Jock Scott'. The Thunder-and-Lightning is a great dark fly, the Logie a great light fly; so is the Silver Grey. But their name is legion. Follow the basic rule and make enquiry locally. The *size*, in my opinion, should never be less than 6/o, and 8/o is better still.

Fishing the sunken fly for salmon is hard work, make no mistake about that. You will soon sweat the muck of winter out of your skin. But I don't know anything much more exhilarating than this fluent labour.

Fish hard, fish slowly, fish deep—and never strike.

And remember that the word 'slowly' applies to *the speed at which the fly moves* IN RELATION TO THE WATER.

CHAPTER 27

Salmon: The Greased Line

Everything that lives is mysterious, fishes more than most, and the salmon is the most mysterious of fishes. I kid you not.

Nobody really *knows* exactly why, but it is a certain fact of Nature that the behaviour of salmon in fresh water changes radically when the water warms up.

The critical temperature—of the water, not the air —seems to be just forty-eight degrees Fahrenheit.

When the river water is below this temperature salmon lie deep and can be taken only on a big deep-fished lure.

When the river-water temperature rises above forty-eight degrees salmon will rise to take a small fly fished very near the surface.

Why? Well, as I say, nobody would go into a witness box and swear he *knew*, for *sure*. But the most ingenious theory to fit the case has been developed by Mr. Richard Waddington, who plunged the entire salmon-fishing fraternity—no, community is a safer word—deeply into his debt when he wrote *Salmon Fishing: A New Philosophy* (Peter Davies, 1947) and *Fly Fishing for Salmon* (Faber, 1951). Mr. Waddington doesn't have to be *right*; but he has evolved a theory which seems to fit the facts of the salmon's odd behaviour, and this theory gives the angler an intelligent basis to work on.

Without which, you are merely flogging the water aimlessly, mechanically, and superstitiously.

Everybody knows that the change occurs when the water warms up. Mr. Ernest Crosfield and Mr. A. H. E. Wood of Cairnton both evolved methods of catching salmon in summer. (Until this century, salmon fishers simply gave up when the river got warm.) But it was left to Mr. Waddington to evolve the theory that seems to make the practice of greased-line fishing in summer not only effective but also rational. Not merely rule-of-thumb empiricism, a sort of opportunism; but coherently arising from a study of cause and effect. Right or wrong—and it is only guesswork, as Mr. Waddington is the first to admit—it makes greased-line fishing twice as interesting, to put it at the lowest.

Fig. 51. The A. H. E. Wood Knot (for attaching fly to leader).

Very briefly, Mr. Waddington's theory is that salmon follow the eels. Eels live the same cycle as salmon, but in reverse. Spawned in the depths of the Sargasso Sea, they come to Europe as tiny things, run up the freshwater rivers to feed and grow large, then vanish back to the Sargasso when the sexual urge bids them reproduce their kind.

The theory is that salmon feed largely on the letocephalus or immature eel. That in winter, in cold water, the salmon is accustomed to taking an elver some three inches long, but that in summer, in warm water (possibly the Gulf Stream) the salmon is accustomed to taking a tiny elver, about an inch long.

This theory is not watertight: the temperature scale and the size scale do not agree. But it is something to work on. Since it is generally agreed that salmon feed in fresh water out of habit, *when reminded of conditions in which they have been accustomed to take food in the sea*, it would seem to make sense that in cold, deep water the salmon may be attracted by a three-inch creature fished deep, whereas in summer (and generally in shallow water, the rivers having run down to summer level) it goes for something smaller and fished near the surface.

Whether this theory is fanciful or a brilliant guess does not matter to us one whit. The fact is that when the water temperature is below forty-eight degrees the salmon can only be interested in a big lure fished deep. When the water is above that temperature it can be attracted only by a smaller lure fished only just below the surface.

I don't mean that if the water temperature rises momentarily to forty-nine degrees the salmon changes over. It might, say, be forty-seven degrees at ten o'clock on an April morning, fifty degrees by 3 p.m. the same day, and down again to forty-five degrees during the night. No. The *average* temperature has to get to forty-eight degrees or above and stick there for several days before the salmon changes over. But once this happens, change over he does—and you must change over with him, or not one fish will you touch.

There is no halfway house. It is absolutely useless to fish a medium fly at mid-water. It is all or nothing— for the salmon, and therefore for the salmon fisher. Below and above that water temperature, the salmon behaves like two entirely different fish.

(It has been known, in Scotland, for the water temperature to fall drastically, *after* it had settled above forty-eight degrees and after everybody had gone over to summer fishing. Until someone cottoned on to this, nobody was touching a fish. One man rumbled what had happened, changed back to cold-water methods, and began to catch fish immediately on a big fly fished deep. Soon everybody followed suit, and there was a 'little spring' lasting a week or so during the summer. Similarly in late autumn, the temperature of the water may get down well below forty-eight degrees. If it does, back you go to 'spring' methods again.)

Now this summer fishing, as I said, is something fairly new—only about half a century old. The credit for inventing greased-line salmon fly fishing belongs to Mr. A. H. E. Wood, of Cairnton water on the Aberdeenshire Dee. But Mr. Ernest Crosfield also caught fish in high summer—by using different methods which achieved the same object, more or less. So did the great Pashley.

And that object is, as you have heard—to fish a small fly right up in the water, barely sunk, in fact. Apart from the fact that it is often desirable to fish the small fly slowly, you will see that the method is radically different from sunk-fly or 'spring' fishing.

It involves totally different gear, to begin with. The fly fisher must always begin with his fly, and work back to the rod. Since the greased-line fisher's fly is a tiny thing about one inch long, very light as to hook-metal, it fishes best on a fine leader—which, in any case, is imposed on you by the clarity of summer water. This leads us naturally to a light line—as light as possible, since it must float perfectly, and the lighter a line is, the better it floats. The whole chain of reasoning ends in a lighter rod.

Some anglers fish the greased line, in fact, with a trout rod, which is perfectly feasible if the water is not too big and wide. Usually, I should say, on any but small rivers, the light, well-balanced, double-handed rod is easier and pleasanter to use. The hollow fibreglass twelve-foot rod is a very useful weapon, the hollow tubular-steel rod of about eleven feet is another. The best rod for this purpose which I have ever held in my hands is the thirteen-foot 'L.R.H.' rod designed by the late L. R. Hardy. But, as I say, many fine fishers manage very well with a single-handed trout rod of about ten feet. Many nine-foot salmon rods are in use today.

The low-water salmon fly is a very different proposi-

tion from the deep-sunk meat-hook of evil memory.
Slight, slender, light in the wire, sparse in the dressing.
That is the conventional low-water fly. There is
another sort, short, fat in the body, often dressed on a
double short-point hook—the 'bug' type of fly. Each has
its devotees: I prefer the slender, in fact *thin*, fly.

Mr. Wood is credited with having laid down a lot of
rules, which many greased-line anglers follow slavishly.
Some of these so-called rules he did not lay down at
all; he has had zealous disciples who have elevated his
slightest remark into the category of gospel. Others
were applicable only to his extremely peculiar water at

FIG. 52. A typical Low-water Salmon Fly (the Logie).

Cairnton. But one thing he definitely did say, and it is
a golden rule anywhere. He said: 'The basic size is
No. 6.'

Now, whereas in spring fishing, with the big sunk
fly, minor variations in size matter little—though it is
in fact advisable always to stick to an 8/o fly—in
greased-line fishing in summer very minute changes in
size mean all the difference between success and failure. The basic size is No. 6, yes: but almost infinitely
small variations, down to No. 10 and up to No. 1, will
make a huge difference.

To put it baldly. In water of medium pace, at a
water temperature of fifty-two to fifty-four degrees, use
the No. 6. If the next pool or stream you try is flowing
faster, put your size UP. If the water is flowing more
slowly, put your size DOWN.

You must aim to hit on the right size. It is vital.

That is practical politics. But, in fact, the salmon is not interested in these minute variations. Why on earth should he refuse a fly nine-sixteenths of an inch long, and grab a fly five-eighths of an inch long? It doesn't make sense. (Though it happens.) One explanation is that the salmon is not really a bit interested in sizes—he is only interested in *a fly that swims at a certain distance below the surface of the water*. This distance must be exactly right for him.

(A theory is that the fly must be sunk just so far that it, and its reflection on the surface, coincide. If it is fishing too deep or too shallow, the actuality and its reflection are seen as two separate and alarming things. A good, intelligent theory, since the salmon is definitely looking upwards, and to him the surface beyond his cone of vision is a mere reflection of the bottom.)

Now it follows that a fly which keeps station nicely in fast water, fishing, say, three inches or two inches below the surface, will fall away in slack water, hanging down and fishing too deep. Conversely, a very small, light fly which fishes at the right depth in slack water will skate, or ride too high, in fast water. And there is an infinity of graduations to be considered. It is the weight of the fly, in conjunction with the area which it presents to the water, plus the speed of the current, that decides how high it fishes.

That is why you start with a basic No. 6 and vary the size of your fly according to the speed of the water you are fishing. In a variable pool containing fast, slow, deep, and shallow water you may have to change your fly several times.

There are other factors. If the water is coloured you may confidently use a fly a size or two bigger than you would otherwise use. If it is particularly clear you drop a size.

The No. 6 basic fly as laid down by Mr. Wood is about right for water temperature of fifty-two to fifty-four degrees—normal early summer. In cooler water, raise the size. In hotter conditions, lower it.

There is a strong school of thought which believes that actually all our greased-line flies are much too small—that the salmon would really prefer something two or even two and a half inches long. But conventionally-made flies of such a size cannot be made to stay riding high in the water, even on a greased line *and* leader. They drop right away, hanging almost vertically however smart the current, and look exceedingly unreal to the salmon.

The answer, I incline to think, is the Terror or Demon type of lure, as often used for sea trout and often in salt water. This type of lure—a mere feather, or hackle, on a strand of nylon or gut, with two small hooks in tandem—seems just the answer to me. It has often killed when nothing else would arouse a fish's interest. I think it has a future, and use it myself in calm, clear conditions. In future I intend to try out the squirrel-tail tube fly thoroughly. I know for certain that it has handsomely beaten all other lures on one particular beat.

However, I have given you a résumé of conventional greased-line fly philosophy, though I think it is going a long way round to achieve a result much more simply achieved by the use of long, thin, featherweight lures.

Now for actually fishing the fly. It is simplicity itself. If all the foregoing about fly sizes has put you off, I am sorry. It necessarily sounds complicated. But, believe me, any beginner who can cast a line can catch a fish on the greased line in well-stocked water. Hence the popularity of summer fishing. It is far more difficult to fish the sunk fly effectively. So please don't be deterred.

It is widely believed that Mr. Wood laid it down as sacred law that in greased-line fishing the fly must float down broadside on, inert as a leaf, without a suspicion of drag. This, frankly, is nonsense. In the first place because it is virtually impossible to achieve. In the second place because the fly must have a semblance of life, and that life is conferred on it only by the action of the water on the materials which make the fly—in fact, by modified, slight, controlled *drag*.

People who believe that the fly must float down inert, without drag, also believe that constant 'mending' of the line is also necessary. Well, it would be, indeed, if drag were to be avoided at all costs. 'Mending' you are already familiar with; it means picking up a curve of

Fig. 53. The 'Dandy' Lure.

line and throwing it, or rather *putting* it, aside— upstream if you want to slow the fly down, downstream if you want to speed the fly up. Well, some mending may always be necessary, but there is little doubt in my mind that it is to be avoided wherever possible. However neatly you do it, it disturbs the water—and it is not often necessary, for the simple reason that drag is *not* an unmitigated evil.

You may, in fact, fish the greased line exactly as you would fish the sunk line—that is, cast a long line down and across and let it swing round. *Of course* there will be a bit of drag. It won't put the fish off. Make your cast as long and at as narrow an angle as possible, and the fly will fish slowly over the fish's lie.

Some people are confused because Mr. Wood often fished his greased-line fly slightly *upstream*. This can be explained.

Mr. Wood was also a devotee of the March Brown— a good big March Brown nymph. During the first part of his cast, the fly was drifting downstream just like a

nymph. Then, when it got well downstream and the
current took hold of it, it came across like a small fish.
Splendid! Two flies for the price of one, two methods
combined in one cast! I do it myself whenever I get
the chance.

Now don't be put off by all this contradictory doc-
trine. If you have the chance of fishing for salmon
when the water temperature is safely above forty-eight
degrees—that is, generally, from about the end of
April until August, or even later—then go about it
with confidence. You will find it much less alarming
than it sounds. If you get your fly size right, by trial
and error or by taking local advice, just you press on,
casting slightly downstream and fishing your fly across
just below the surface in the expectation that a salmon
is going to rise and seize it.

What happens then? Well, it is still true that on no
account must you ever strike. If you see signs of the
take, or if your line stops, or if you see the knot where
leader and line are joined *draw* slightly—then all you
must do is throw the salmon all the line you can. Drop
that loop which you have been holding in your left
hand, lower the rod top, pull line off the reel, walk
downstream—anything, to get a big belly of line floating down past the fish. It is the pull of the current on
this belly of line which pulls the hook into the fish's
jaw—preferably right in the 'scissors' of the jaw. If you
strike, you will merely pull the fly out of the fish's
mouth. That's for sure.

This takes some getting used to, and is a severe
strain on the dear old nerves. But it is the only possible way of hooking your fish. Once you have allowed
the big belly of line to form downstream of the fish, he
must be hooked. Then you can reel in and tighten up
at leisure.

Sometimes you will find that a fish rises to your fly
but does not take hold—always an exciting and sometimes an unnerving experience. What to do then?
Change the size of fly. The fish will return to its lie

and have a short rest while you are doing this. If the fish has refused you at the last moment, it is evidence that your fly interested him—therefore, he is in a taking mood—but that at the last moment, when he got close enough, he was disappointed in the lure. In other words, he saw through it. It failed to persuade him. Now if you are fishing fast water, put up the size of your fly. If you are fishing placid water, put it down a size or two. And try again.

Undoubtedly greased-line fishing is terribly interesting and exciting. You often see the fish rise to take—sometimes in a real trout-like head-and-tail rise. Nor is it difficult, once you have struck a fly of suitable size for the circumstances.

Of all fishing, possibly, this is the cream.

I must mention that the same effect can be achieved by using a very light *un*greased line. This was Pashley's way. He never fished the greased line. He used a trout rod and No. 1 line—it didn't sink far, but it sank enough to cut out that deadly shadow—and he fished very fast. Bear that in mind.

CHAPTER 28

High Summer Salmon

Greased-line fishing finally resolves itself, as the temperature rises and the water levels fall, into a fascinating and difficult game of stalking individual salmon with a trout rod.

This is the absolute peak of angling, for if you can get a salmon to take your little fly, cast upstream as to a trout, and then land him on your gossamer gear, you will have known one of the most exquisite, painfully thrilling moments in angling.

In Canada and the United States salmon are caught all summer on the dry fly—a true floater, cast exactly as a trout fly, upstream to individual fish. The fly is usually fuzzy. Many attempts have been made to reproduce this sort of sport in Britain, but not with marked success. True, all the same, that salmon are hooked, every summer, by trout fishers (and a fine surprise they get). True, too, that salmon can be seen to suck in small natural flies, exactly like huge trout, almost any hot summer evening.

It follows that as the salmon get accustomed to their river quarters, as the water level falls and the temperature rises, so ancestral memories seem to return, and they begin to take an interest in the river flies on which they fed in their parr days. This is the time, when the water is low and fine tackle a must, to stalk a fish and try it with a small fly, cast from a trout rod.

Since no one has succeeded in catching salmon *regularly* on the dry fly in Britain, it is no good advising you to try. (Though somebody will always be trying.) What I do recommend, in such conditions, is the old crafty combination of the floating fly and the nymph. I am sure that it can take many more fish than some people think.

With a March Brown wet fly on the point and a hackled dry fly on a dropper, stalk your fish and cast obliquely upstream exactly as you would to a trout.

Since you are stationed more or less downstream of the fish, you can tighten on a riser without waiting so long as the downstream greased-line fisher has to wait.

Another fine, exciting way of fishing is to cast a shrimp fly across river, upstream of the salmon's lie,

FIG. 54. Artificial Fresh-water Shrimp.

and let it come down so that after drifting nicely into the fish's range of vision it suddenly swirls off and heads for mid-stream just before it reaches him. This will often bring a salmon into violent action—and watch out when it does!

Indeed, there are often fish so stale and potted that you get just one chance at them in a day, one and one only. In the early morning, as a rule, or the late evening. Then it is often good policy to cast your fly so that it falls just ahead of the fish's nose—and snatch it away immediately by a tug on the line. This sometimes brings the fish raving to snatch it. Almost any fly, a Terror as well as another.

There are locations, beloved by salmon, where you simply cannot drift a fly down over the lie. In this case it sometimes works to cast your fly so that the belly of the line begins to snatch it across the stream just as it floats down within the salmon's reach. The fly that suddenly changes course and flashes across the fish's nose, broadside on, may waken a sulky fish and impel him to pursuit—angry pursuit, one is tempted to write, though we know so little of a fish's psychology that it is almost impertinent to attribute to them our own failings.

Well, there are dozens of different tactical approaches for the man with the trout rod. It is the greatest fun in the world, at a time when salmon, long potted in shrunken pools, are notoriously almost impossible to catch by conventional methods. Finally, I commend to your notice the method used by the upstream clear-water spinner. He throws his small minnow directly, or almost directly, upstream, and brings it back past the fish's lie at tremendous speed, winding the reel handle like a madman. You can *try* this with a fly, stripping line like a wild thing. Better, though, to get on the blind side of the fish and let the current do the work by dragging your flasher fast past him.

Should you be wondering what it is like to hook a salmon on a trout rod, let me reassure you that it happens hundreds of times every season. I have seen a fifteen-pounder landed in ten minutes on one of Eggington's spliced split-cane trout rods, nine and a half feet in length and weighing barely six ounces. A *pliant* trout rod will master almost any salmon. And what a terrific thrill it is. Shark fishing with a pole and rope is nothing to it, nothing at all.

American anglers have carried the cult for light tackle to fantastic extremes, and salmon are actually landed with 'brook' rods weighing under three ounces. But this is going a bit too far, and is quite unnecessary. You need perfect freedom of mobility, and it is a matter of rushing up and down the bank to keep in touch with your fish. A refined form of cruelty, perhaps. However, I tell you this in order to reassure you about your chances should you hook a salmon on a normal trout rod of nine to ten feet, weighing perhaps five to eight ounces.

The great Pashley of the Wye caught almost all his

incredible number of salmon on a trout rod. An old one.

When the rivers are shrunken, the water really warm, and the salmon ultra-wary, this is your only chance of a fish—and then only at morning and evening. Never travel without your trout rod. It may save a holiday from ruin.

CHAPTER 29

You Can Do It!

I hope that I have not made fly fishing seem too difficult. Even more fervently I hope that I haven't made it sound too easy. Fly fishing is just difficult enough—if you aspire to do a good workmanlike job—to make exactly the sort of demand on your concentration which truly re-creates something valuable and important within you. I consider it a perfect change from the complex world of modern man, the ceaseless war of nerves. It brings me refreshment, and I daresay it will do the same for you. In fly fishing you find a uniquely therapeutic mixture of tranquillity and excitement.

Don't worry if nothing seems to go right on your first outing. Nothing went right with me for years! Well, that's not quite true, but it isn't so very far out. I was brought up in the Black Country, a coarse fisher, a float fisher, ignorant and happy on the banks of dark pit-pools and sluggish brown canals. Fly fishing, when I came to it comparatively late in life, was a new world to me, a heaven of fresh and delightful experiences.

I had to teach myself, without a tutor, and very painful it sometimes was; more than a little humiliating. I stuck at it because I recognised at a glance that this was the summit of the angler's craft. I knew that once mastered it was going to give me huge dividends in happiness. And so it proved.

Some modes of angling are gregarious, and these suit gregarious men. But if you enjoy getting away from your fellow men for a time, slipping away unnoticed into the beautiful loneliness of the unpeopled riverside, then the fly fisher's solitary sport will make the same keen basic appeal to you that it made to me. There is no question of 'superiority' in my mind: I have tried to make it clear that fly fishing is quite easy once you have digested a bit of sound advice. But unlike the placid routine of sitting on a hamper with your friends, fishing the float—and there are times when I love that, too—unlike that simple gregarious pastime, fly fishing takes you off on your own into the wild and lovely places where swift streams run off to sea down the shoulders of the everlasting hills. For this there is no substitute in the crowded world of men.

I have tried to emancipate would-be fly fishers from some of the clinging fetters of 'received authority'—because I remember how it held me back, in my own pursuit of this simple pleasure. There is a little to learn, but there is no need to listen humbly to pontificating bores who lay down the law as if there were only one right way. There are a number of ways, some of which will suit your *temperament* better than others.

If it seems hard sleddin' at first, let me tell you that there will surely come a day when, suddenly, miraculously, it will all become simple, fluent, and joyful. Everything will fall into place, and you will find yourself fishing well and happily without a thought for the mechanics of the business.

My oldest pupil was seventy before ever he held a rod in his hand. He turned out very well. His only regret, of course, was that he didn't try fly fishing sixty years before.

And there it is. You go on, living and learning to the end. Good luck to you. Think of me sometimes when you feel that indescribably thrilling tug as a fish takes hold and the rod leaps in your hand.

East Clandon, 1957.
Cranleigh, 1965.
Stoke Bliss, 1976.

Further Reading

TROUT
> *Thoughtful Practice with a Dry Fly*. Arthur Woollcy.
> (Redman.)
> *Fishing Ways and Wiles*. H. E. Morritt. (Cape.)
> *Keeper of the Stream*. Frank Sawyer. (A. & C. Black.)

SEA TROUT
> *Fishing for Sea Trout*. H. P. Henzell. (A. & C. Black.)
> *The Floating Line for Salmon and Sea Trout*.
> Anthony Crossley. (Methuen.)
> *Sea Trout Fishing*. Hugh Falkus. (Witherby.)

SALMON
> *Salmon Fishing: A New Philosophy*. Richard Wad-
> dington. (Peter Davies.)
> *Fly Fishing for Salmon*. Richard Waddington. (Faber
> & Faber.)
> *Angling Conclusions*. W. F. R. Reynolds. (Faber &
> Faber.)
> *My Way with Salmon*. Ian Wood. (George Allen &
> Unwin.)

SALT WATER
> *Salt Water Angling*. Michael Kennedy. (Hutchinson.)

COARSE FISH
> *This Fishing*. L. A. Parker. (Bennett.)

FLIES
> *An Angler's Entomology*. J. R. Harris. (Collins.)
> *Fly Dressers' Guide*. John Veniard. (E. Veniard.)

GENERAL

Anglers' Fishes and their Natural History. Eric Taverner. (Seeley, Service.)

Wandering Fisherman. V. Fox-Strangways. (Arthur Barker.)

Still-Water Angling. Richard Walker. (David & Charles.)

Index

NAVIGATION

A. C. GARDNER

Navigation does not have to be the province of the specialist alone, and there is no reason why anyone who possesses a minimum of mathematical knowledge should not master the basic theory and principles from this book. The author, himself a highly qualified navigator at sea and in the air for twenty years, explains in simple language the techniques, instruments and calculations used in all kinds of navigation with the aim of giving the general reader a thorough grounding in the subject. A brief history of navigation is also included and there are many helpful examples and exercises.

TEACH YOURSELF BOOKS